SOLD OUT

How an American magazine lost its soul

Stuart Englert

Copyright 2015© by Stuart Englert
All rights reserved.

Except as permitted under the U.S. Copyright Act of 1976, no part of this publication may be reproduced, distributed, or transmitted in any form or by any means, or stored in a database or retrieval system, without the prior permission of the author. Requests should be submitted to Sold Out, 21 Vaughns Gap Rd. H141, Nashville, TN 37205.

Printed in the United States of America
First Edition: January 2015
Cover photo and design by Stuart Englert

Library of Congress Cataloging-in-Publication Data

Englert, Stuart
Sold out: how an American magazine lost its soul /
Stuart Englert

Summary: "Journalist Stuart Englert chronicles the inspiring and spiritual founding of American Profile magazine and the publication's gradual decline as editorial and ethical considerations succumb to pressure for short-term profits and the influence of advertisers amid economic recessions in the United States."

ISBN: 978-1505834116 (paperback) :
1. American Profile—United States 2. Magazine publishing—United States 3. Media ethics—United States 4. Business ethics—United States 5. Main Street—United States 6. Wall Street—United States

To truth seekers

ACKNOWLEDGMENTS

Special thanks to Dan Hammond for his inspiring story and cooperation, Marta Aldrich for her encouragement and suggestions, Martha Malloch for her precious support, and my parents for imparting me with the audacity to question authority and conventional wisdom.

CONTENTS

Introduction ix

Section I: SPIRITUAL BIRTH

Chapter 1	Divine Guidance	5
Chapter 2	Defining Moment	10
Chapter 3	Capital Adventure	16
Chapter 4	Good News	22
Chapter 5	Uninvited Guest	28

Section II: MONEY IS GOD

Chapter 6	Integrity Undermined	35
Chapter 7	Changing of the Guard	40
Chapter 8	Monetize Editorial	43
Chapter 9	Howdy Partner!	46
Chapter 10	Yes Men	50

Section III: FLYOVER COUNTRY

Chapter 11	Adoring Readers	57
Chapter 12	God, Family and Country	62
Chapter 13	Sense of Belonging	65
Chapter 14	The Great Divide	71

Section IV: ADVERTISING RULES

Chapter 15	Calling the Shots	77
Chapter 16	Big Pharma	83

Chapter 17	That's Entertainment 88
Chapter 18	Double Standards 92
Chapter 19	Damn the Firewall 101

Section V: DEVIL IN THE DETAILS

Chapter 20	Behind the Façade 107
Chapter 21	Ever-Shrinking Magazine 110
Chapter 22	Austerity Measures 114
Chapter 23	Window Dressing 119

Section VI: DIGITAL DIVIDE

Chapter 24	Twisted and Tangled Web 127
Chapter 25	Robots vs. Humans 134
Chapter 26	Breakdown Breakup 141
Chapter 27	Severing the Roots 146
Chapter 28	Some Things Never Change . . . 152

Afterword 159

INTRODUCTION

In 1982, while attending an introductory journalism class at Indiana University, I asked Richard Gray, a professor and dean of the School of Journalism, if a private business enterprise, such as a newspaper, could be socially responsible.

Gray declined to answer the question at the time, telling the class "we'll get to that later." Gray, who was arrested in 1984 on a Tampa, Fla., beach on charges of lewd and lascivious conduct, resisting arrest and battery on police officers, never answered my question. However, I found an answer 30 years later while working as an editor of *American Profile*, the "good news" magazine distributed to 10 million homes and businesses each week. I discovered that when a publisher is driven solely by the profit motive, readers take a backseat, credibility is compromised, and the pages—as well as the soul—of a magazine are for sale.

In short, some publishing companies perceive that it's unnecessary or not in their best interest to be responsible—or responsive—to readers. Quarterly earnings are more important, and to meet financial goals, unscrupulous publishers allow advertisers and search engine analytics to dictate and influence editorial policy and content. In the 21st century, it's a miserable and sad reality of the American media.

Sold Out is a story about how the short-term quest for advertising revenue, lack of editorial scruples, and a cadre of yes men and women cost a magazine its integrity and soul.

Section I
SPIRITUAL BIRTH

*

"Advertising is the priority, profitability is the objective, and we'll do anything to get to profitability," declared Executive Editor Charlie Cox on June 6, 2003.

While Cox later clarified his statement prohibiting any illegal acts, it was clear that ethical boundaries would be crossed and journalistic principles would be violated in American Profile, the "good news" magazine launched in Nashville, Tenn., four years earlier.

Under Cox's directive, the top concern of editors no longer was assigning stories and photos to attract readers. Rather, the primary focus was catering to companies willing to buy an ad in the newspaper-distributed magazine. The contention was that to be financially successful, the magazine had to make some unsavory choices and compromise its editorial mission of "celebrating the people, places and things that make America great."

Along the rocky road to riches, small-town readers took a backseat so big-city advertisers would fill the tank that kept the publication's engine running. "The readers are just a speed bump on the way to profitability," said editor Richard McVey in 2005, sarcastically describing the magazine's readership as more of an obstacle than an asset.

No longer was American Profile merely a magazine; it

had become a public relations tool for advertisers with money to spend.

Yet, the publication wasn't born exclusively of financial interests. Its origins were admirable and praiseworthy. In fact, its founder attributes its birth to guidance from and faith in God.

Chapter 1
Divine Guidance

L. Daniel Hammond conceived the idea of *American Profile* in 1991 after speaking with Maynard Davis, a commercial printer and business associate in Nashville. Davis wondered why newspaper inserts, such as *Parade* and *USA Weekend*, weren't distributed in small-town newspapers.

"I know exactly why those magazines aren't distributed in small towns," said Hammond, then vice president of marketing at Comdata, an electronic payment processor in Brentwood, Tenn. "There are not enough of us. We don't make enough money" to support magazine distribution to rural areas of the country.

"You oughta just go think about that," replied Davis, waggling his finger at Hammond, 31 at the time, married with one child and another on the way.

Hammond took Davis' advice. He began researching newspaper-distributed magazines, including *Family Weekly*, founded in 1953. The magazine was purchased by Gannett Co. in 1985 and renamed *USA Weekend*. He also studied the philosophy and business models of Walmart founder Sam Walton and Al Neuharth, the founder of *USA Today*, which in 1982 became the first newspaper to use computers and satellites to transmit stories, photos and pre-press pages, permitting daily nationwide distribution.

Other than the fact that *Parade*, founded in 1941, and *USA Weekend* had been serving large, urban daily newspapers for years—even decades—Hammond couldn't find a compelling reason why those magazines weren't distributed in small-town daily and weekly newspapers.

"The daily newspaper people think that weekly community newspaper people are redheaded stepchildren from the backwaters," said Hammond, an Indianapolis native who grew up in Noblesville, Ind. "And the folks at the 8,000 community newspapers think that the journalists and owners at urban daily newspapers don't have a lick of sense about their audience."

So, Hammond surmised, if *Parade* and *USA Weekend* had built their businesses predicated upon serving metropolitan dailies, filled with news about gang violence, teen-age pregnancy and crack-addicted babies, and they started catering to small-town weeklies, which featured stories about Little League baseball, high school class reunions and the county fair, they were going to face a clash of cultures. In identifying the fundamental differences between the nation's two largest demographic sectors—urban and rural—Hammond discovered the basis for creating a magazine specifically for the latter.

It was an epiphany of great proportions. Hammond had stumbled upon a "rock solid" opportunity that demanded attention. Plus, he knew a startup company could launch a new magazine much quicker and at a fraction of the cost of a large corporation such as Advance Publications, publisher of *Parade*, or Gannett Co.

To develop his idea, Hammond, Davis and two other business associates—Adele Rowan and Steve Rogers—met a few hours a week for a couple of years to strategize; address printing, logistical and distribution concerns; and formulate a business plan for the magazine. They formed a partnership and, with about $40,000 contributed by Hammond and Davis, hired a ghostwriter to polish their final business plan. "I mortgaged my house," recalled Hammond, noting that his wife was pregnant with their second child at the time. "Once we finished with that process, we knew we could do this," he said. "We knew we could make money. In fact, it had the potential to be very big."

With their grand plan for *American Profile* in hand, the team went on the hunt for investors. In 1993, the group met with a couple of local investment bankers who arranged a meeting with Massey Burch, then the only venture capital firm in Nashville, and its president Don Johnston, who was impressed with their proposal.

"I see hundreds of business plans," Johnston told Hammond. "Yours is among the best I've ever seen."

Dumbfounded, Hammond recalled asking himself, "How can that be?"

Johnston said he didn't know anything about magazine publishing, but he would be interested in talking further—and possibly funding the venture—if Hammond and his team could find a couple of industry veterans to validate the viability of their plan.

By happenstance, within a week, Hammond and his brainstorming colleagues all went their separate ways and their partnership dissolved. Hammond landed a lucrative job in Minneapolis, where his brother lived; Rowan was offered a partnership in her publishing company; Rogers bowed out to pursue the priesthood; and Davis didn't have the drive to singlehandedly chase their magazine dream.

Davis and Hammond decided to let another publisher give their idea a whirl. They offered the business plan to Rex Hammock, founder and CEO of a custom media and marketing services company in Nashville, and Albie Del Favero, publisher of the *Nashville Scene*, with the understanding that they'd get the plan back if the magazine wasn't launched within five years.

"I handed off years of blood, sweat and tears," said Hammond, fearing he may have let a fortune slip through his fingers.

Chapter 2

Defining Moment

Money long had been Hammond's motivation for starting a business. All that the aspiring entrepreneur needed was an idea to believe in.

"When I was doing those business plans, I was doing it for one reason; I saw the scale and size of this business," he said. "I loved the marketing opportunity and I could be rich."

In the back of his mind, he recalled what a former client had said to him early in his marketing career. "You know what the difference is between guys like us and guys who start businesses?" the client asked Hammond. "They've got *cajones*." Hammond remembered thinking to himself: "I've got *cajones*. I've just never seen or found an idea that made me enough of a believer to risk everything."

He believed in the idea of publishing a magazine for small-town newspapers, but he didn't have the money to finance the venture. In 1994, Hammond accepted a high-paying job in Minneapolis to feed his growing family. Within a year, he lost the job. He had just built a new home and suddenly found himself on the verge of bankruptcy. "I couldn't find a job to save my life," he said, recalling that he was unemployed for 2 ½ years.

His wife, Cherie, suggested he do some soul-searching. "She said I did not have the Lord in my heart," Hammond recalled. "On a 1-to-10 scale as a believer, I was about a 2."

After repeatedly having doors closed by prospective employers, Hammond was downtrodden and worn out. He had nowhere else to turn, so he turned to God. "I started believing and it changed my heart," he said.

Shortly thereafter, he got a call from a business associate in Tennessee, asking him to return to Comdata. "It was like manna from heaven, and I jumped at it," he said. "Within a month, I felt the Lord's hand on me, and he told me that I was supposed to pick up that old business plan and rewrite it."

The thought left Hammond in disbelief. He didn't understand how he could simultaneously perform his new job and resurrect the idle business plan. Plus, he was flat broke, had a mountain of debt and his family remained in Plymouth, Minn., where his wife was impatiently waiting for their home to sell. "How in the world am I supposed to do that?" wondered Hammond, who was living in an apartment in Brentwood, a Nashville suburb.

Soon the answer became clear. Hammond must quit his job and dedicate himself to starting the magazine. He returned to Minnesota for a weekend visit, not revealing to his wife that he was contemplating quitting his job. On that visit, his wife volunteered that the Lord had placed another message in her heart, which greatly piqued his interest, considering the divine guidance he recently had received.

"She said to me, 'You're not putting the Lord first.'"

"I said: 'No, no. Look what we've gone through. Look at how I've changed.'"

She replied, "No, I'm talking about tithing."

An infrequent churchgoer and sparing contributor to the collection plate, Hammond laughed and said: "That's an old Jewish law by an old Jewish king."

She responded: "I told you what I heard. You need to go think about it."

Hammond returned to Tennessee. For two weeks he read every passage he could find in the Bible about tithing. All he could find was that it's a good thing to do. "It's recommended; it's not mandated," he said, believing that giving 10 percent of one's income to the church was open to interpretation.

On a subsequent visit to Minnesota in 1997, Hammond and his family attended Speak the Word, an evangelical church in Golden Valley, Minn., led by pastor Randy Morrison. "I was sitting in the pew and the minister said 'Turn to Malachi chapter 3, verse 10,'" Hammond recalled. "So I turned to it and it stunned me."

"Bring the whole tithe into the storehouse, that there may be food in my house," the passage reads. "Test me in this, and see if I will not throw open the floodgates of heaven and pour out so much blessing that there will not be room enough to store it."

"At that point, the minister said, 'This is the only passage in the Bible where God challenges us to test him.'"

Hammond sat in the pew flush from the revelation. He asked his wife for an index card that she kept in her Bible for taking notes. With pen in hand, he deducted 10 percent of his salary, along with his monthly mortgage payment and bills. "And the math doesn't work. There is no way to do this," he said to himself, recalling the spiritual guidance he had received weeks earlier in Tennessee.

It was a defining moment in Hammond's life. In the depths of his heart, he accepted the divine challenge and vowed to begin contributing 10 percent of his income to the church and charitable causes—despite uncertainty about how he would pay the family's bills.

On the drive home, Hammond handed his wife the index card and they both burst into tears. "She's crying because she's happy; I'm crying because I'd lost my mind." When they arrived, a phone message from their real estate agent revealed that their home had been sold at their asking price, plus the buyer wanted to purchase all of their appliances. A huge financial burden had been lifted. At that moment, Hammond knew he had to return to Tennessee to pursue his business plan. "I have a mission," he said. "I know this business is going to happen."

Hammond believed he was on the right path and pursuing the business for the right reasons. Miraculously, his family's debts seemed to evaporate. With their home in Minnesota sold, the entire Hammond family returned to Tennessee to start life anew and pursue Dan's mothballed magazine idea.

During a visit with Bill Brennan, co-founder of Mailnet Services in Nashville, Hammond was introduced to Steve Young, a Mailnet executive who'd been selling brand advertisements in rural markets across the nation. Hammond and Young realized an immediate connection. They agreed to scrutinize the business plan and discovered that technological advances had made *American Profile* more viable in 1998 than it had been eight years earlier. "We validated the business models and plans and we agreed we were going to do it," he recalled.

Hammond and Davis, his former business associate, retrieved their unfulfilled plan from Hammock. They agreed that Davis would receive a 20 percent stake in the company while Hammond, as the driving force, would get 80 percent. Hammond quit his job at Comdata and Brennan provided him with office space at his Nashville business.

His grand idea had entered its incubation stage.

Chapter 3

Capital Adventure

With renewed confidence, Hammond once again set out to find financial backing. In 1999, he and Young traveled to Boston to meet investors with the Megunticook Fund, a venture capital firm. "We bowled them over," recalled Hammond, remembering that Young impressed the New England financiers with his knowledge of the origins and meaning of their company's name, which in the Algonquin Indian language, refers to a place in coastal Maine that means "big mountain harbor." Tom Matlack, Megunticook's managing partner, kept writing "good" on his paper as Hammond and Young unveiled the details of their business plan.

Hammond was down to $700 in his bank account when he and Young began final negotiations with their Megunticook backers. Ultimately, they agreed on a $3.5 million investment, allocated in two tranches and contingent upon meeting several advertising and circulation milestones. To get a head start on meeting those targets, Hammond once again mortgaged his home. He used the money to hire Nashville-based marketing and public relations firms, Creative Works and Katcher Vaughn & Bailey, to develop promotional materials, including an *American Profile* prototype aimed at celebrating the good news in hometown America.

The prototype's cover featured a photo of a playful circus clown. Inside, stories profiled the Hugo, Okla.-based Kelly Miller Circus and the Circus World Museum in Baraboo, Wis.; the covered bridges of Rockville, Ind.; and a family doctor in Belleville, Wis., who made house calls to see his patients.

S.A. Habib, founder of Creative Works, was uncertain if his staff could meet the stringent production deadlines for the magazine's prototype, media kits and other marketing materials. Hammond tried to allay his concerns, saying, "You have to trust me on this. You are actually going to do this. It is going to so amaze you."

With his enthused employees working late into the night to complete their assignments, Habib began to see evidence of Hammond's prediction. One night, he called Hammond to inquire, "What is it about this? I've never seen anything like this."

"God is in this," Hammond replied.

"He must be, because I cannot get my staff to even go home," Habib responded.

SOLD OUT

While *American Profile* was being readied for launch, Hammond tried to maintain a low profile for his startup, Publishing Group of America (PGA). He didn't want to attract the attention of established media giants—particularly Advance or Gannett—fearing they might attempt to commandeer his fledgling company or sabotage it by offering to serve small community newspapers. "We had to be a submarine," he said. "No one needed to know what we were doing."

Hammond fathomed that stealth would provide an insurmountable advantage for his emerging enterprise. "By the time we surface and they realized we do have torpedoes, it's too late, we're up and running," he said, continuing his submarine analogy. "At that point, they will have to make a decision. Do they board her and try to take her over, do they try to sink her or do they let her live? Boarding her and taking over would signal that the idea was sound, fighting her—'Well, good luck'—because I knew that we would build a better magazine and would do a better job serving our readers and newspaper partners."

Simultaneously, while the marketing materials and prototype were being readied, Hammond began interviewing and hiring employees to sell and produce the magazine. Soon ads promoting *American Profile* were run in trade magazines such as *Advertising Age*, *Adweek*, and *Editor & Publisher*. Apple pies draped in red gingham cloth were delivered to a hundred media buyers in Chicago, Detroit, Los Angeles and New York. And newly printed marketing materials were mailed to every weekly and small-town daily newspaper in the nation.

During PGA's first board meeting, members inquired how Hammond and his team had accomplished such a feat. Pointing to Hammond, Young replied: "Dude, took a mortgage on his house months ago when we started the negotiations." Awestruck board member Heb Ryan responded: "Oh my God! These guys have just laid their swords on the table."

Hammond's energetic team exceeded every funding prerequisite and, in late 1999, the company received the second portion of the Megunticook investment, plus an additional $4 million from individual investors, for a total of $7.5 million. "Within three months, we had surpassed the hurdles in front of us," Hammond said. "We closed on the additional financing and got on with running the business full-bore."

During the National Newspaper Association Convention in Boston in October 1999, information packets about *American Profile* were slid beneath the hotel doors of every conference attendee. Small-town publishers and editors were abuzz with the prospects of a full-color magazine produced specifically for their newspapers.

Hammond gained immediate support from some of those publishers during a dinner conversation. While seated at a table with a dozen or more newspaper executives, one of them asked, "What ads will you not accept in your publication?" Hammond responded: "We won't take liquor ads. I don't think we'll take tobacco ads, and we won't take a Walmart ad." The publishers, many whom had similar restrictions on alcohol and tobacco ads in their own papers, gave him a rousing round of applause. Plus, his position on Walmart, the retail giant that had decimated hundreds of small-town business districts, aligned with their own. "Walmart killed many of the mom-and-pop businesses in these small towns that were their mainstay advertisers," Hammond said. "And Walmart doesn't advertise in their papers."

In Hammond, small-town publishers had found a kindred spirit.

His conviction and enthusiasm were contagious, and his employees—sensing that they were part of a momentous endeavor—fervently embraced their assigned tasks. Seven salespeople set about signing up hundreds of newspapers to carry *American Profile* while a handful of eager editors scoured the nation for stories and photographs that celebrated hometown life.

The energy required to launch the magazine resounded throughout PGA's offices as circulation sales reps rang a Mississippi State steel cowbell each time a new publisher contract was in hand, a tip of the hat to Young, the company's senior vice president of sales and a Mississippi State graduate. Meanwhile, Young and his ad sales staff began garnering contracts and commitments from advertisers, some who paid more than $140,000 for a full-page brand ad.

Chapter 4
Good News

On April 23, 2000, *American Profile* officially launched, with 1.2 million copies of the tabloid-size magazine distributed via 250 daily and weekly newspapers in 24 states across the Midwest and Southeast.

While some media prognosticators were predicting the death of print, the homespun, general-interest publication debuted as one of the most successful magazine launches in U.S. history just as the Internet was reaching critical mass and the much-hyped Millennium Bug failed to disrupt the Digital Age. The magazine's impressive debut and pioneering approach caused quite a buzz across the media world.

"I've been reviewing magazine launches for 15 years and *American Profile* is one of the top five launches I've seen in the last few years," said Samir A. Husni, professor of journalism at the University of Mississippi. "The magazine is filling a void for weekly and small daily newspaper publishers with a distribution channel that simply did not previously exist."

The 16-page newspaper insert found an adoring audience in small towns across America where its big-city competitors, *Parade* and *USA Weekend*, had failed to venture. Its stories—about hometown life and heroes, charming communities and traditions, and easy-to-make recipes—resonated with readers.

"I love it—the weekly features, special articles, recipes, everything," gushed Marjorie Sherman after her hometown newspaper, the *Palmyra* (Mo.) *Spectator*, distributed *American Profile*'s inaugural Midwest edition. The Easter issue featured stories about the allure of hometown America, the Tulip Time celebration in Pella, Iowa, and the charitable acts of a Wisconsin teenager, as well as a folksy cartoon called *Able County* and an egg salad recipe.

Within a year, circulation had rocketed to 2.8 million—distributed via 560 newspapers across the 48 contiguous states—and Husni, a media consultant and researcher known as Mr. Magazine, had bestowed *American Profile* with his 2000 Launch of the Year award, along with *O*, Oprah Winfrey's magazine. "Knowing your audience and providing them with great content will always be a successful formula," Husni said about *American Profile*. "The Publishing Group of America took this advice to heart."

American Profile's recipe for success was filling a media niche based upon a three-legged stool—advertisers, readers and newspapers—the latter providing a distribution network for the magazine. With its attractive four-color photos and design, the magazine supplied a steady stream of "good news" to mostly black-and-white community newspapers and their loyal readers while providing national advertisers with a new vehicle to reach underserved markets in rural America.

Advertisers provided roughly 90 percent of the magazine's revenue, while "publishing partners"—the daily and weekly newspapers that carried the insert—contributed the remainder to defray printing and shipping costs. Thanks to advances in printing technology, logistics and distribution, the model worked.

Within a year of the magazine's launch, PGA had received an additional $23 million in venture capital from Quadrangle Capital Partners of New York City to expand nationwide. *American Profile* grew to five regional editions—Midwest, Southeast, Northeast, Central and West. The media brand had taken root in America's heartland.

As its staff approached 50, the company relocated its corporate offices from Nashville to a larger space in nearby Franklin, Tenn., and launched a website, *americanprofile.com*, which mirrored the print magazine.

Friends and critics who had warned Hammond that good news wouldn't sell were proven wrong.

"The people that work here gotta believe that hometown America is an important fiber in American life," Hammond told the *Nashville Business Journal* in 2001. "They must have a bias for morality, so that whether they're selling it, shipping it or writing it, they're not faking it."

Most of Hammond's employees didn't have to fake it; they believed in his vision of celebrating the values and virtues of living in hometown America—far from the glitz and glamour, fashion trends and passing fads promoted by Hollywood and Madison Avenue. *American Profile* didn't mimic the sensationalism of *National Enquirer*, disseminate celebrity gossip like *People*, or publish the bloodshed and political scandal plastered across the pages of *Time* and *Newsweek*. That's why the editorial mission of "celebrating hometown life" proved so popular among publishers and readers.

Unlike its metropolitan counterparts *Parade* and *USA Weekend*, *American Profile* was a healthy slice of American pie, akin to a hybrid of *Grit* and *Guideposts*. Its uplifting stories about average Americans doing extraordinary things for others and their communities were like a refreshing breath of country air amid a pervasive blanket of inner-city smog.

Each of the magazine's five editions contained stories unique to the geographic area where it was distributed, including a Hometown Hero and Hometown Spotlight; a state-by-state regional events calendar called Happenings; a state-by-state regional trivia column dubbed Tidbits; and regional recipes. A cover story explored human-interest topics of national interest, while a one-page Q&A column called Ask American Profile featured reader-submitted questions about their favorite celebrities.

"Refrigerator Journalism USA" is how *Editor & Publisher* described the magazine. "No doom and gloom for *American Profile*," the trade publication proclaimed as Hammond and his magazine were heralded by other media, including *Advertising Age*, The Associated Press, *American Demographics*, *American Journalism Review*, the *Chicago Tribune*, CNN and *Forbes*.

The magazine's success also caught the attention of two Harvard Business School professors, who used PGA's company history and private equity financing as a case study that they presented to their students. When Hammond traveled to Boston in 2002 to answer student questions about his startup, he stopped at a

Harvard bookstore to buy souvenirs: a ball cap for himself and school pennant for his father. "I attached a note to the pennant and mailed it to my dad. I wrote: 'Hey Dad, I'm the first Hammond to go to Harvard,'" recalled the 1982 graduate of Miami University in Oxford, Ohio.

Hammond's American dream was coming true.

Chapter 5
Uninvited Guest

Hammond envisioned and promoted a publication with high advertising and editorial standards. Shunning the star-studded content of most mainstream magazines, he preferred to pay tribute to average Americans, even prohibiting celebrities on the cover unless they were demystified and linked to hometown America. He likened *American Profile* to "an uninvited guest" in the homes of readers; he didn't want the magazine to intentionally offend or upset them by publishing salacious or unsavory stories.

Known to scrutinize the magazine's pages before they were sent to the Quebecor World printing plant in Dickson, Tenn., Hammond sometimes questioned the selection of stories and images. In the fall of 2000, for example, he ordered replacement of a photograph of cleavage-exposed country music artist Jamie O'Neal in an ad promoting her debut album. "We're not running that photograph. It's too risqué," he told ad salesman Frank Zier. "Go back to her publicist and get a different photo."

To keep the magazine family-friendly, Hammond prohibited overtly sexual ads, even excluding bra advertisements as tacky and unattractive. When brand advertising was slim, *American Profile* filled empty pages with public service ads from non-profit organizations such as the Association of American Publishers to encourage reading by American youth and the Partnership for a Drug-Free America to discourage illegal drug use.

The high-road approach worked in community newspapers. Jerry Lyles, PGA's director of circulation, said small-town publishers liked that the magazine mirrored their communities and validated their values. "*American Profile* reflected what's great about small towns and the country," said Lyles, a native of a Mayfield, Ky. "It made them proud about where they live."

To avoid direct competition with *Parade* and *USA Weekend*, Lyles and his sales team initially focused on signing up small-town weeklies to carry *American Profile*. The magazine wasn't free. Newspapers paid $20 to $50 per 1,000 copies, depending on their circulation. The higher their circulation, the lower the cost. The magazine's "publishing partners" incurred other costs as well. Those without presses often paid the printer to insert *American Profile* into their papers, and all spent more to mail the magazine to subscribers who received their newspapers via the U.S. Postal Service. Conversely, Advance and Gannett *paid* metropolitan dailies $10,000 to $100,000 a year to distribute *Parade* and *USA Weekend*, with fees based upon a newspaper's circulation.

The contrast in business models left some in the publishing industry scratching their heads. Hundreds of small-town publishers, nonetheless, were willing to pay for *American Profile* because its editorial content represented their own communities and readers. "They sent us a couple of copies and one had a feature on a family dairy farm," Bill Randolph, publisher of the *Harrodsburg* (Ky.) *Herald*, told The Associated Press. "It's about the common, everyday man."

Regional content also was appealing. "The regionalized component of this publication is very exciting to us," said Nancy Bliss Slepicka, publisher of the *Montgomery County News* in Hillsboro, Ill. "Unlike non-regional national publications, with *American Profile* there is a strong likelihood that readers have personal knowledge of the people and places profiled in the magazine."

The magazine also provided small-town publishers with distribution flexibility. Unlike its big-city counterparts that circulated only on Sunday, *American*

Profile could be inserted into newspapers any day of the week.

Overall, it was a winning formula. A 2006 survey found 98 percent of publishers were "very satisfied," "somewhat satisfied" or "satisfied" with *American Profile*, while only 2 percent were "not satisfied" with the overall magazine and its editorial quality. On a scale of 1 to 5, they rated the magazine's cover stories (4.2), Hometown Spotlight (4.2), Hometown Heroes (4.1) and Made in America (3.9) features as most important to their readers. Meanwhile, the celebrity column rated 3.6, equal to the quality and type of advertising in the magazine.

The response from weekly newspapers was so positive that *American Profile* began targeting dailies in towns with populations of 85,000 or less. By 2008, *American Profile*'s circulation had climbed to 10 million, ranking the humble—and often unheard of among city dwellers—publication among the nation's top five largest magazines and making it nearly as large as *People, Newsweek* and *Sports Illustrated* combined.

Takeaway: Prophets seldom dwell on profits.

Section II
MONEY IS GOD

*

"The price of freedom can be dear, as it was to so many of those who dared sign their names to the document declaring this a free land," stated the July 1-7, 2001, American Profile *cover story about the risks taken and sacrifices made by the nation's founding fathers.*

Titled "The Patriots," the story detailed how 13 of the men who signed the Declaration of Independence in Philadelphia on July 4, 1776, lost their lives, families, fortunes and estates for defying British rule of the American colonies.

"Firm and decided as a patriot, zealous and faithful as a friend to the public, he loved his country, and adhered to her cause in the darkest hours of her struggles against oppression," *the story concluded.*

*

Chapter 6
Integrity Undermined

Despite his best intentions to publish a family-friendly, wholesome magazine, Hammond from the outset had to face the realities of making *American Profile* profitable. Though he initially opposed tobacco ads in the magazine, for financial reasons he succumbed to Big Tobacco's deep pockets and accepted ads for one of the nation's most popular and addictive legal drugs: nicotine. The inaugural issue included a Doral cigarette ad.

The ad troubled some publishers who didn't permit tobacco advertising in their own newspapers. "We only had two choices: distribute *American Profile* or send it back," said Michael Williams, editor and publisher of *The Paris* (Tenn.) *Post-Intelligencer*, who cancelled his subscription in 2001, citing cigarette ads. "We have no other control over the magazine's advertising policies."

Hammond and his sales representatives assured concerned publishers that they would seek other national advertisers to replace the tobacco ads. However, cigarette ads ran in 17 of the magazine's first 18 issues. "We needed it," Hammond said matter-of-factly, conceding that the magazine probably wouldn't have survived without revenue from tobacco giants Brown & Williamson, Philip Morris and R.J. Reynolds.

Cigarettes and smokeless tobacco ads became commonplace in the magazine. Within its first six years, *American Profile* published more than 100 tobacco-related ads, including a few from Philip Morris that offered information on how to quit smoking. Despite sporadic complaints, Hammond justified running the ads because most publishers didn't cancel their subscriptions. "The newspaper publishers didn't have an issue with them," he said. "If they did, we wouldn't have run them."

Confronting moral and fiscal challenges, it didn't take long for the early and infectious optimism of Hammond and his team to run head-on into the single-minded focus of advertising and accounting executives hired to turn *American Profile* into a moneymaking machine, particularly as some financial backers desired a rapid return on their investment. And just as the magazine was garnering praiseworthy attention and accolades, the attacks of Sept. 11, 2001, dealt a severe blow to the national economy, American psyche and advertising expenditures.

While conceptually and strategically *American Profile* was a remarkable success, the ill-timed launch of the magazine was unfortunate and unforeseeable. The economic slump that followed the bursting of the dot-com bubble and 9/11 was devastating to the U.S. publishing industry as manufacturers and retailers reduced advertising spending. Some magazines—*Mademoiselle*, *McCall's* and *PC/Computing*—ceased publication, while others cut staff and costs to weather the economic recession. As advertising revenue declined, publishers were forced to tighten their belts and find creative ways to keep the presses rolling.

PGA wasn't immune to the upheaval. To reduce expenses in 2002, *American Profile* was reconfigured, eliminating content unique to each of its regional editions—Hometown Heroes and Hometown Spotlights—and the need for five regional editors. The company's first staff layoffs ensued and the magazine's stories became national in scope, though regional trivia and events calendars remained.

Under pressure to turn a profit, some company executives began to question the magazine's economic viability and members of the ad sales staff, led by Tracey Altman, increasingly offered editorial favors in exchange for advertising. Altman, who joined PGA as vice president of advertising sales a month after *American Profile*'s launch, gained a reputation for incorporating product mentions in stories and promising health-related articles to pharmaceutical companies. The former ad director and publisher for American Media, owner of *National Enquirer* and *Star*—supermarket tabloids that specialize in celebrity gossip and scandal—claimed to support the magazine's editorial mission even as she worked to undermine it. Each time Altman and her sales team granted a favor to an advertiser, they knocked the company's three-legged stool off balance, threatening to tarnish or taint the *American Profile* brand. Readers and newspaper publishers always came up on the short end.

In 2002, Coty ran an ad in *American Profile* to promote a new fragrance called American Original. "She is one of a kind and she makes a difference," the ad touted in the magazine's Mother's Day issue. As part of the ad campaign conceived by Hammond and implemented by Altman, readers were offered a chance to nominate a woman who they considered an American original. Entrants were told one winner would receive $2,500 and the nominee's story would be featured as a Hometown Hero in *American Profile*.

Linda Broadhead, of American Falls, Idaho, won the contest and received the cash prize. However, the story she wrote about her pioneering and beloved mother,

Nona Rogers, never appeared in the magazine. "She had an extraordinary life," said Broadhead about her mom who died in 2012. "She drove a semi and carried bombs during World War II."

Broadhead called the magazine several times to inquire why the story wasn't published. She never received a legitimate answer. She was so disappointed that *American Profile* had broken its promise to publish the story that she canceled her subscription to the *Power County Press*, which carried the magazine.

The very integrity that *American Profile* celebrated in its stories was undermined.

Chapter 7
Changing of the Guard

Financial demands and managerial disputes led to turnover and turmoil among the company's executive ranks. In November 2002, with the board's directive, Hammond hired Dick Porter as publisher of *American Profile* and senior vice president of PGA to strengthen the company's ad sales team. Porter previously was publisher of *TV Guide, Reader's Digest* and *Prevention* magazines, and most recently had worked for AOL Time Warner. Two months later, Hammond was abruptly removed as CEO, and Young and at least a dozen other employees—mostly editorial and production staff in Nashville—were laid off. They soon were replaced with advertising and marketing personnel in the company's New York City office.

While Hammond retained his position as chairman of PGA's five-member board, he no longer supervised or managed the company's day-to-day operations. CFO Stephen Duggan attributed Hammond's departure to "a difference of opinion" with the board of directors. Unbeknownst to Hammond, Duggan had convinced other members of the board to cut a third of the magazine's staff to enhance PGA's financial position in preparation for the company's sale. Hammond opposed employee layoffs. Moreover, he wanted more time to grow the business before putting it on the market. He noted that PGA was on the verge of profitability and had money in the bank. He suggested that selling the 3-year-old company was premature. "What you are doing is wrong," he told the board. "It's not going to work out."

According to Hammond, board member Peter Ezersky, managing principal at Quadrangle, responded: "You know what my problem is with you? You're too nice. You treat your people like rock stars. You should be beating the shit out of these guys."

Hammond was, in fact, a gracious and generous boss. He appreciated the hard work, talents and contributions of his employees, and wanted them to be recognized and compensated accordingly. For helping him start one of the nation's most successful magazines of 2000, Hammond rewarded staff with $500 gift certificates during a launch party, stock options and yearend bonuses. PGA also initially paid 100 percent of employee health insurance premiums and provided a dollar-for-dollar match of 401K contributions. *American Profile* was a great place to work under Hammond and most of his employees admired and respected him.

Hammond's departure was peculiar. He said the board didn't have legal grounds to terminate him, and that he voluntarily stepped down as CEO to avoid a lengthy court battle that could have greatly harmed or destroyed the company. "I was actually the only one acting in the best interest of all shareholders and stakeholders," said Hammond, PGA's single largest independent shareholder. "I didn't want to see the company ripped apart over greed."

Porter immediately replaced Hammond as CEO, Duggan became PGA's chief operating officer, and Altman took over as *American Profile*'s publisher. Porter, who lived in New York City, vowed to carry on Hammond's legacy, telling employees that he understood and embraced family and small-town values. His empty words soon proved hollow. Almost immediately, Porter was focused on quarterly profits and addressing the company's bottom line, and the importance of the magazine's partner newspapers and readers became secondary.

Chapter 8
Monetize Editorial

Without Hammond at the helm, *American Profile*'s grand slide down the slippery ethical slope accelerated. Within a month of being named CEO, Porter suggested that the magazine "monetize editorial" by offering complimentary articles to advertisers, mentioning their products in stories and showing them in photos.

Executive Editor Peter Fossel did his best to comply with Porter's directive, requesting a story about Battle Creek, Mich., also known as Cereal City USA, for a breakfast edition. The goal was to garner advertising from food companies such as Kellogg's, and the payoff was a Kellogg's Eggo syrup ad published adjacent to the story. Fossel, using the pen name Zach Thomas, also wrote a summer picnicking tips story, which mentioned that "Dole now offers pineapple chunks, peaches and tropical fruit in lightweight, unbreakable 24-ounce plastic jars." An ad promoting Dole's jarred products appeared below the story.

In June 2003, to celebrate Ford Motor Co.'s 100th anniversary, a story titled "Henry Ford—The Man Who Changed America" was published. The story was accompanied by a four-page Ford advertisement, reportedly valued at $250,000, along with a reader sweepstakes for a trip for two to The Henry Ford museum and village in Dearborn, Mich.

American Profile also used its Tennessee connections to leverage advertising from Nashville record labels. In hopes of putting *Country Weekly* out of business and garnering $2 million in annual advertising from country music labels and companies that wanted to identify with the Nashville entertainment industry, PGA executives requested extensive country music coverage, including 12 stories a year about country artists and icons.

To pave the way, Fossel was terminated and Beverly Keel, a Nashville-based *People* magazine contributor, was hired as entertainment editor to spearhead the country music initiative. While the plan appeared brilliant since country music is particularly popular in rural areas, it detracted from the magazine's mission of spotlighting average Americans and violated Hammond's restrictions on celebrity coverage.

After eight music-related cover stories in six months, including articles about George Strait, Willie Nelson, Alan Jackson, Reba McEntire and Kenny Chesney, *Country Weekly* remained in business, and some newspaper publishers in the Northeast pushed back, noting that they never intended to carry a country music magazine. In response, the magazine diversified its celebrity coverage to include entertainers in other musical genres as well as media and political figures.

By requesting "product shots" and "star quality" on the magazine's cover, Porter led the effort to detour the editorial mission. Furthermore, he justified breaching the firewall between advertising and editorial functions. "All the media are doing it, including AOL Time Warner," he said during an editorial meeting in February 2003.

During a subsequent meeting with editors, Altman passed around the June 2003 issue of *Ladies Home Journal,* which featured Celine Dion on the front cover and an advertisement on the back cover promoting the singer's new namesake perfume. "This is what Tracey is up against," Porter declared.

Ad salesmen and marketers had taken over the reigns of the company, the magazine's editorial mission had been rerouted and go-along to get-along editors helped grease the skids.

Chapter 9

Howdy Partner!

Similar to its country music initiative, PGA found another way to attract advertisers, breach the firewall and alter the magazine's editorial mission. Company officials formed "partnerships" with the Professional Rodeo Cowboys Association (PRCA), National Rural Health Association and Kansas City Barbeque Society. The objective was to garner ad revenue from the groups' sponsors and other advertisers who wanted to reach a rural audience interested in bronc-riding competitions, high blood pressure and hickory-smoked cuisine.

Dodge and Wrangler, for instance, were official sponsors of the PRCA. So in 2004 and 2005, *American Profile* published 10 rodeo-related and Western-themed stories to secure ads from those heavy-duty brand advertisers. In one issue, a Dodge Ram truck ad was sandwiched between a story about PRCA's Wrangler National Finals Rodeo. A Wrangler denim jeans ad appeared on subsequent pages. Some readers and non-rodeo fans likely wondered why the magazine had suddenly gone cowboy crazy. Only its rodeo "pards" knew for sure.

Meanwhile, ads for Bush's Best baked beans and Cattlemen's barbecue sauce appeared alongside "Smoke, Sizzle & Sauce," a cover story about barbecue cook-offs since the Kansas City Barbeque Society each year sanctions hundreds of the events across North America.

Porter nurtured relationships with broadcast media as well, convincing them that the magazine could boost their viewership in the Heartland. In hopes of gaining attention, ad revenue and prestige, *American Profile* in 2004 partnered with Fox News Channel to publish a four-part Democracy in America series. Fox anchors and hosts David Asman, John Gibson, Sean Hannity and Brit Hume wrote forwards for stories titled "Liberty Lessons: What does freedom mean to our children?"; "Being a Good Citizen: What do Americans think about citizenship?"; "The Right to Vote: First-time voters voice their views"; and "Freedom's Responsibilities: Four generations of military veterans tell what it means to serve their country."

While the stories were genuine and meaningful, and featured people in communities where *American Profile* was distributed, the messages seemed out of place adjacent to ads for penis pumps and sexual dysfunction supplements. Or insincere when a health story required by an advertiser displaced a Hometown Hero story.

American Profile also developed relationships with other cable and TV networks, promoting shows and personalities for ABC, CBS, CNN, NBC, CMT, Discovery and Hallmark Channel to garner advertising. In 2004, *American Profile* profiled CBS' Charles Osgood; in 2005, CNN anchor Bill Hemmer; and in 2006, Tim Russert, host of NBC's *Meet the Press*, and Brian Williams, NBC news anchor. An ad for the *NBC Nightly News* ran in the issue immediately after the Williams' story, and cable and TV networks purchased dozens of other ads in exchange for promotion of their shows and movies.

Not all readers were impressed with the magazine's ties to Big Media. "Please don't include The Peacock," wrote Laura Estes of Odessa, Wash., referring to NBC's logo on an eight-page promotional pullout in 2008. "It detracts from the hometown flavor of *American Profile*. We get enough political news and trash celebrity news in the dailies. Keep *American Profile* a source of good news, happy news from ordinary people."

During board meetings, Hammond questioned the shift toward celebrity-driven stories. His concerns, however, were met largely with indifference and shrugs from other PGA executives. "They treated me like an ignorant rube," he recalled. "Clearly, they cared little about the readers or newspaper publishers who distributed the magazine."

Chapter 10
Yes Men

Most editors and writers compromise their ethics and principles on occasion to support a belief, idea or cause—or to retain their jobs. When ethical compromise becomes the editorial policy of a publication, the slippery slope rapidly steepens. Cox, who assumed the executive editor's position following Fossel's departure, greased the slope in 2003 when he declared: "We'll do anything to get to profitability." The company's former production director, Cox assumed the top editorial post though he had little experience as an editor.

Actually, cooperation between the advertising and editorial departments wasn't new—or unlawful in any way. Some may argue that it's a perfectly legitimate business practice, especially as a favor to regular advertisers or during tough economic times.

The practice in the pages of *American Profile* began discreetly and innocently, with a single story accompanying an ad to accommodate or appease an advertiser. The inaugural issue, for instance, included a story about ways to avoid summer allergy symptoms on the same page as a Kleenex tissue ad and, in the next issue, a Ritz crackers ad appeared below a story about road-trip snacks for kids.

But over the years, the practice mushroomed until advertisers controlled or influenced thousands of pages of editorial content, displacing stories that complied with the magazine's evolving mission "to celebrate the people, places and things that make America great." Editorial "tie-ins," as the compromised and questionable content was called, increased in frequency and duration until pharmaceutical companies received up to a half-dozen stories a year mentioning the health disorders or diseases treated by their products.

American Profile published enough drug, tobacco and entertainment-related ads in 2003 to turn its first quarterly profit. More than a dozen of those ads "monetized editorial" as Porter had suggested. An Adderall ad, for example, was accompanied by a story titled "Detecting a Learning Disability." The drug is used to treat children diagnosed with attention deficit hyperactive disorder (ADHD). "Maintain a Healthy Heart" appeared on the same page as a Tylenol ad, which said "Taking a low-dose aspirin a day for your heart can be a smart thing to do. Taking a pain reliever that won't interfere with it is even smarter."

SOLD OUT

In its back-to-school issue, a "Buying a Computer for College" story was published adjacent to an ad for a Compaq computer and Hewlett-Packard (HP) printer. In a Christmas issue three months later, a HP digital camera and color copier were plugged as "Great Gift Ideas for Your Family" in an Our Picks column adjacent to a HP ad. Altman reportedly provided the copy.

As advertising revenue increased, some issues of *American Profile* appeared to be cover-to-cover advertorials. By 2004, nearly two-thirds of the magazine's 52 issues had stories linked to ads, with up to four in a single issue.

Privately, Cox opposed the repeated editorial tie-ins, though he seldom expressed that opinion in staff meetings. The former creative director for the defunct retailer Service Merchandise previously supervised the printing of catalogs, and it was apparent he wasn't the kind of man to question the ethics and decisions of his superiors. He was the consummate yes man, which helped explain why he was appointed executive editor despite having limited editing credentials.

Other employees endorsed or tolerated the influence of advertisers.

"What does it matter?" art director Brennan Sharp chimed in on the merging of advertising and editorial functions. "We're a fluff magazine."

Sharp added: "We had to do it" to get profitable. "We didn't have a choice."

Cox doubted that most readers noticed the links between ads and stories. Some readers did, however. "As a former journalist, I was disturbed to see your article on osteoporosis placed opposite an ad for an osteoporosis medicine," wrote Joan Feldman. "Tsk! Tsk! Doesn't lend much credibility to the other stories you publish when the ideas come from sponsors/advertisers."

Ralph, a reader from Minnesota, also questioned the proximity of health stories and pharmaceutical ads. "You have very good and informative stories on diabetes and osteoporosis, but why do they have to be backed up by a drug ad? Why do they have to tie together?"

Attempting to calm dissension from subordinate editors, Cox said: "It will be a different ballgame" once the magazine is profitable, suggesting that the pressure to pamper advertisers—and assist ad sales reps— would diminish once adequate revenue was rolling in.

"We're almost there," he said after two consecutive months of net profit.

Dissenting editors, however, weren't convinced, particularly since Cox usually complied with Altman and Porter's editorial requests. Furthermore, Cox had suggested that *American Profile*'s readers really didn't matter—as long as newspapers continued to distribute the magazine.

Editors who cared about the readers also doubted the appetites of Madison Avenue media buyers would be satiated once they had tasted the sweetness of editorial favors. They also noted that during companywide staff meetings, financial matters dominated. Porter introduced advertising initiatives and Duggan announced fiscal results, while the magazine's stories, readers and partner newspapers were seldom discussed.

Money, it seemed, had become God at PGA and *American Profile*.

Takeaway: Few of today's publishers and editors would make great patriots.

Section III
FLYOVER COUNTRY

*

"While growing up in Mount Airy, N.C., Andy Griffith never wanted to be an actor. He wanted to be a preacher instead," wrote Beverly Keel in 2005 after interviewing the most popular celebrity ever profiled in American Profile.

Griffith's beloved TV character, the caring small-town sheriff and devoted single father on The Andy Griffith Show, best epitomized the hometown values celebrated in the magazine.

"In retrospect, the show served as a vehicle for Griffith to preach his message of knowing right from wrong to his TV audience," Keel wrote. In similar spirit, American Profile shared good news from small towns that resembled Griffith's fictional community of Mayberry, N.C.

*

Chapter 11
Adoring Readers

Reminiscent of a Norman Rockwell painting or one of Charles Kuralt's "On the Road" segments on the CBS television network, *American Profile* featured stories about genuine and kind-hearted people, interesting and off-the-beaten-path places, and innocent and simpler times that gave readers hope for humanity and the nation.

While some PGA executives considered the opinions of bumpkins in flyover country—the vast swath of the United States between the metropolitan Northeast and Southern California—inconsequential as long as their newspapers continued to distribute the magazine, those same readers adored *American Profile* for its inspirational and homespun stories. "Just wanted you to know how much I enjoy your *American Profile* magazine—all the stories about the little town people," wrote Elizabeth Pedrick of Stevensville, Md.

From the outset, *American Profile* received dozens of calls, emails and letters from readers each week, most praising the magazine's positive and decent content and appetizing recipes. "In a world with so much bad news all around us each day, your magazine is like a breath of fresh air and an encouragement with its positive and faith-lifting articles. Keep up the good work and may God bless your efforts," wrote Alice Wilson of Spokane, Wash.

While a venture capitalist in Washington, D.C., once had told Hammond that good news wouldn't sell—and that magazines had to include sex, drugs and alcohol to be successful—*American Profile* readers consistently offered a different opinion. "Just had to write and let you know what a pleasure it is to read your upbeat magazine," wrote Jackie Marconi of Pasadena, Md. "I'm very tired of 'celebrities,' crime and scandals. Yours is a welcome bright spot in my newspaper. Thanks for publishing it."

Some readers claimed to read the magazine before they perused their own community newspapers, and occasionally they compared *American Profile* to its metropolitan counterpart, *Parade*. Most asserted—or implied—that the new kid in town was superior to its older, big-city cousin. One Michigan reader was disappointed when his local newspaper stopped carrying *American Profile*. "What your reasoning was for replacing *American Profile* with *Parade*, I don't know, but I would seriously consider changing newspapers to get it back," Buzz Jelinek of Harbor Springs, Mich., wrote in 2007 to the editor of the *Petoskey* (Mich.) *News Review*. "You replaced a wonderful, uplifting magazine with a second-rate gossip magazine."

Readers regularly urged the magazine to maintain its small-town flavor. "*American Profile* truly reflects America, not New York City and Hollywood," wrote Melvin and Evelyn Getz of Rockville, Md., in 2007. "We enjoy everything about this publication and look forward to receiving it every week. It reminds us of the America we grew up in and love. Please keep *American Profile* just as it is."

Whether they were nostalgic, patriotic or poignant, stories that tugged at the heartstrings elicited the greatest response, such as the 2002 cover story titled "A Job for Jimmie Brennan." The story described how a gasoline station owner in Higginsville, Mo. (pop. 4,682), took a chance in 1967 to hire a developmentally disabled man. As a result, Brennan became a longtime employee, a faithful friend and beloved citizen in the community.

Especially popular were feel-good vignettes in the annual "Acts of Kindness" feature, in which readers shared accounts of compassionate and generous deeds performed by friends, neighbors and strangers. "So glad our newspaper includes *American Profile* with our semi-weekly paper," wrote Joanna Michaels of Franklin, N.C. "The Acts of Kindness story makes for must reading. It gave a warm feeling in a world that isn't smiling or laughing very much it seems."

American Profile published hundreds of Hometown Hero stories about altruistic and benevolent individuals who devoted their time and talents to charitable and humanitarian causes, or assisted their fellow citizens and the less fortunate. Among the selfless subjects were caring coaches, compassionate doctors, generous farmers, devoted teachers and philanthropic business owners. One touching story profiled P.K. Beville, founder of Second Wind Dreams, which fulfills wishes for elders living in nursing homes and assisted living centers in and around Marietta, Ga. Another featured Tiffany Grant, founder of Prom Wishes, which provides formal dresses and tuxedos to Oklahoma teenagers who can't afford to buy or rent them for their ceremonial high school dances.

The articles proved so popular that *American Profile* in 2007 published a paperback book, *Hometown Heroes: Real Stories of Ordinary People Doing Extraordinary Things All Across America*, which featured profiles of 50 praiseworthy people. "If your faith in humanity has sagged, this book is for you," Phillip Gulley, a Quaker minister and author in Danville, Ind., wrote in the forward. "It probably won't change your life. But it will cause you to remember the Light of Human Goodness that cuts through the gloom."

Chapter 12

God, Family and Country

American Profile was one of the few mainstream publications willing to mention God or cover issues of faith. The magazine printed stories about George Washington's religious beliefs, Nativity scene collectors, preservation of North Dakota's prairie churches and a circuit-riding preacher in rural Montana. Readers praised the stories and sentiments, noting that spiritual issues were conspicuously absent in most of the mass media.

"First, I want to thank you and your entire staff at *American Profile* for finally giving the citizens of these United States a weekly publication that is truly representative of the majority of us who still love God, family and country! Sometimes I feel that we are the 'forgotten people' by much of the news media," wrote Marjorie B. Provan of McKeesport, Pa., in 2007.

Family matters were a large part of *American Profile*'s DNA as well. The magazine regularly published stories about Mother's Day and Father's Day, longtime married couples, adoptive and foster parents, family reunions, genealogy, and multi-generational family farms and businesses.

God, Family and Country

A story about the famous Kansas sextuplets born in 2002 turned into a tale of an extended family of faithful volunteers—all grandmothers—who helped parents Sondra and Eldon Headrick feed, burp, bathe, diaper, cloth, cuddle and rock their three boys and three girls four days each week.

When it came to patriotism, *American Profile* was true-blue. The magazine celebrated national loyalty in rural and small-town America with stories about the nation's founding fathers; the nation's oldest and largest flag maker, Annin & Co. in Roseland, N.J.; and Waterloo, N.Y., the birthplace of Memorial Day. After the attacks of Sept. 11, 2001, the magazine published "A Symbol of Freedom," a story about the U.S. flag, along with a two-page pullout of Old Glory that readers posted on walls or in windows as a symbol of national pride and support. The backside included excerpts from the U.S. Flag Code detailing display etiquette.

Photos of the Stars & Stripes were commonplace on the cover of *American Profile*, and a single star marked the end of every story. Editors and page designers rejoiced in the number of times that the red, white & blue flew—both intentionally and unintentionally—on the magazine's pages.

SOLD OUT

American Profile honored the nation's military veterans with stories about William Crooks, of Mount Vernon, Ohio, one of the last surviving World War I pilots; Honor Flight, the non-profit organization that takes World War II veterans to Washington, D.C., to view the national memorial honoring their service; and Morrill Worcester's annual Christmas wreath-laying project at Arlington National Cemetery in Virginia.

"Remembered Soldiers, Forgotten War," a 2006 Veterans Day story, evoked memories among Korean War veterans. The story detailed Ron Broward's 55-year search for Warren "Jackson" Rarick, his childhood friend and fellow U.S. Marine, who went missing on the battlefield in 1951.

"It was so good to see *our* war get some attention, especially since it was the war with the most missing and prisoners of war," wrote Dee James of Tionesta, Pa. "Thank you again for giving Korean veterans, and the most worthy work of Ron Broward, the spotlight. As much as a swabbie hates to admit it, he is one heck of a Marine."

Chapter 13
Sense of Belonging

Reader affection for *American Profile* spanned beyond love of God, family and country to the very heart and soul of the nation. Because most of the articles were about average Americans, readers identified with the subjects, embraced their stories, and gained a sense of belonging and trust in the magazine.

To most readers, the magazine was about them—or people like them—and the places they lived or one day hoped to visit. Among people profiled were barbers and birdwatchers, Girls Scouts and grandparents, pastors and pet owners, Civil War re-enactors and members of the Red Hat Society.

The magazine's Hometown Spotlights crisscrossed the countryside, taking readers to Bemidji, Minn., and the headwaters of the Mississippi River; Lexington, Mass., birthplace of the American Revolution; Mark Twain's hometown of Hannibal, Mo.; West Yellowstone, Mont., on the doorstep of Yellowstone National Park; and hundreds of other well-known and little-known communities.

American Profile allowed elderly and homebound readers to get a glimpse of the United States without packing a bag or boarding a plane. "Your magazine takes me so many places, and I don't even have to leave home," said Rose Greulich of Ferdinand, Ind.

Because home-cooked meals, family dinners and church potlucks are a large part of small-town life, one of *American Profile*'s most popular features was Reader Recipes. Thousands of readers submitted handwritten and typed instructions for making their favorite foods, along with photographs of themselves, for publication in the magazine. The idea for Reader Recipes dawned on editors in 2000 after they found it time-consuming to obtain original recipes every week for each of the magazine's five regional editions. By soliciting them from cooks across the country, *American Profile* obtained a varied and steady stream of salads, soups, entrees, side dishes and desserts from ordinary Americans. The recipes created a connection with readers, and gave them a chance to have their names, photos and anecdotes published in a national magazine.

American Profile published its first Reader Recipe—Oatmeal Cake with Penuche Frosting from Sharon Altman, of Pekin, Ill.—in its July 15, 2001 issue. "This recipe was my mother's and has become a favorite of our son, Scott, who is an astronaut," Altman wrote.

"When he visited us recently, I sent this cake home with him. It rode well in the T-38 plane for his quick trip back to Houston."

A litany of recipes—and personal accounts—followed, such as those for Craisin Salad from Audrey Misner of Price, Utah; Potato Soup from Donna Viola of McPherson, Kan.; Curry Chicken from Fran Tucker of Canisteo, N.Y.; and Peanut Butter Fudge from Drema J. Holstine of Gay, W.Va.

"I have cooked all of my life as a hobby, because I like to eat good food," wrote Bill Carlton of Ruidoso, N.M., who offered his No-Fail Pot Roast recipe. "I invite several couples to Sunday dinner, and this roast is one of their favorites. The secret ingredient is the chili powder."

With hundreds of family- and staff-tested dishes in its database, *American Profile* in 2004 compiled 40 of its best into a spiral-bound cookbook, *Hometown Recipes Vol. 1*. It was the first of more than a half-dozen cookbooks published by PGA, including *Hometown Cookbook: A Celebration of the American Table*; *Hometown Recipes for the Holidays*; and *Hometown Get-Togethers: Memorable Meals for Great Gatherings*. Readers gobbled up hundreds of thousands of copies.

In addition to printing their recipes, editors engaged readers by soliciting and publishing personal accounts about their mothers, grandparents, marriage proposals, favorite teachers, hometowns, first cars, best friends, unique names and uncommon collections.

In 2003, when *American Profile* asked readers for anecdotes for a Mother's Day story, nearly 1,000 responded with heartfelt letters describing what makes their moms great. "She was the one person I could count on, and I knew she loved me unconditionally, even when I didn't love myself," wrote Marsha Sichting of Blackfoot, Idaho.

"Mother's greatest gifts to her children were how she taught us to love by taking the smallest portion on the plate for herself, returning 'too much' change to the grocery, and sitting in the middle of the car seat so we could have the window. Mother taught us about washing our hands, behaving in public, and loving God," wrote Linda. F. Thomas of Beaumont, Texas.

When *American Profile* in 2006 posed the question "What makes your hometown great?" readers from across the nation responded with pride. Rhonda Corchado claimed no strangers live in Lyons, Colo. (pop. 1,585), and that friendly residents have very strong arms. "When you drive down the road and wave, you just leave your arm out the window in one continuous gesture," she said.

The 2007 story "Will You Marry Me?" related the many ways and places that readers or their spouses had popped the question. In "My First Car," readers shared humorous and memorable tales about drivers' examinations, drive-in movies and quirky mechanical malfunctions. "What's Your Name?" detailed the origins and meaning of readers' unusual monikers such as April May March, Blue Hothouse, Comfort Covers and Heaven Leigh Friend. And in "Best of Friends," readers detailed their most cherished friendships through life's ups and downs, joys and sorrows.

Editors also solicited photographs from readers who submitted thousands of images that exemplified the nation and its people for the magazine's "My America" photo contest. Harold Ogden of Tahlequah, Okla., won $500 and first place in the inaugural 2006 contest for his photo of a red barn and its stunning reflection in a Vermont lake. Second place captured the sweet embrace of a son and his returning-soldier-father, and third place featured an image of fireworks exploding over South Dakota's Mount Rushmore. The contest's iconic images of barns and bald eagles, cowboys and American Indians, majestic mountains and scenic rivers captured the beauty and vastness of the countryside from sea to shining sea.

While publication of uplifting stories and beautiful photos from average Americans in a magazine with nationwide reach was rare, *American Profile* broke the mass media mold, creating a personal connection with its readers and providing thousands of them with clipped keepsakes to share with family and friends, press in scrapbooks or post on their refrigerator doors.

Chapter 14
The Great Divide

The sentimental stories and simple recipes in *American Profile* were unlike those published in most large-circulation magazines. The difference was intentional based on Hammond's marketing insights and editorial vision. That's because rural Americans are distinct from their urban and suburban counterparts.

People in small towns and rural areas own more gas grills, guns, lawnmowers and pickup trucks per capita, while urbanites devote more of their income to housing, clothing, education and public transportation. Small-town folks are more apt to plant gardens and eat home-cooked meals; city dwellers spend more on carryout food and restaurants. Urbanites generally are more socially liberal; country folk more religiously conservative. Small-town voters lean Republican; metropolitan voters increasingly cast ballots for Democrats.

Forging a bond between the two was like forcing a square peg into a round hole or getting all members of Congress to see eye to eye, particularly since Madison Avenue, the hub of America's advertising industry, is in New York, the nation's largest city, and worlds apart from Podunk USA.

Hammond, a Republican, confronted the political differences between urban and rural America during a pointed exchange with Quadrangle co-founder Steven L. Rattner, a Democratic fundraiser and later President Barack Obama's car czar. Rattner questioned the wisdom of Tennesseans after the 2000 presidential election in which Texas Gov. George W. Bush, a Republican, defeated Vice President Al Gore, a Democrat from Carthage, Tenn.

"We were in a board meeting in New York, and right in the middle of the meeting Rattner says to me, 'I've got a question for you. What's up with Tennessee?'" recalled Hammond, who responded: "I'm sorry, I don't understand what you mean."

Rattner, who was on Gore's short list for U.S. Treasury secretary, said, "Why wouldn't you vote for your own guy?"

Hammond replied: "You're asking the question backwards. Not only didn't Gore win Tennessee, he didn't even get the support of the people in his own congressional district, and where we come from that means his own momma didn't vote for him."

The Great Divide

Gore would have won the election had he carried his home state, regardless of extensive media coverage of Florida's ballot controversies and subsequent recount. But based on Rattner's question, the Wall Street financier whose company invested $23 million in *American Profile* clearly didn't understand the Main Street mindset—at least in GOP-leaning Tennessee.

With demographic and statistical research in hand, PGA's ad sales staff was acutely aware of the cultural, social and political differences between rural and urban Americans. Advertising and marketing agencies often take those differences into account when devising national ad campaigns. Based on Nielsen Corp.'s population classifications, Americans who live in small towns and rural areas inhabit C and D counties, while their urban and suburban counterparts live in A and B counties, respectively. The biggest challenge for the ad sales team was convincing brand advertisers of the significant purchasing power of people in C and D counties and the benefits of advertising in *American Profile*.

The task was particularly difficult because media buyers in New York City and Chicago generally consider the small towns where the magazine is distributed part of "flyover country." Metropolitan ad agents and marketing executives who ride the subway and work in skyscrapers understandably have a tough time comprehending the lives and interests of consumers in Goodland, Kan.; Hazard, Ky.; Big Timber, Mont.; Oil City, Pa.; or Sweetwater, Texas.

Despite the great divide between folks surrounded by sun-drenched farmland and media buyers who bask in the glow of Broadway's marquee lights, *American Profile* survived. To do so, the magazine's ad sales team consistently sought to bridge the gap or alter editorial content to appeal to Madison Avenue.

Takeaway: Madison Avenue is a long way from Mayberry, N.C.

Section IV
ADVERTISING RULES

*

"Bob Burns may be the most ordinary person in America. He's 54, married, wears glasses, makes mortgage payments on a three-bedroom ranch-style house, and works 40 hours a week as a maintenance supervisor at Windham Technical High School in Willimantic, Conn. (pop. 15,823)."

"The job can be a handful, like any job," Burns told American Profile's contributing editor Marti Attoun in 2006.

Burns drinks coffee each morning, reads the newspaper each day, walks his dog each evening and attends church most Sundays. The 5-foot-8-inch father of three is such an average Joe that he was the unpretentious star of the 2005 book The Average American: The Extraordinary Search for the Nation's Most Ordinary Citizen, *authored by Kevin O'Keefe, whose two-year nationwide journey and statistical research led him to Burns.*

When ordinary Americans like Burns read American Profile, *most got a good feeling about the magazine and the nation. What they likely didn't know was the seedier side of publishing a national magazine and the publishing industry's general disregard—and distain—for people and places that are considered average.*

*

Chapter 15
Calling the Shots

While the magazine's endearing and uplifting stories appealed to ordinary Americans, advertisers ultimately ruled. Because ad revenue paid most of PGA's bills, *American Profile* increasingly was diverted from its editorial mission of celebrating hometown life. With ad sales reps and media buyers calling the shots, the magazine took on the reptilian trait of a lizard that changes color to blend with its surroundings—one week resembling a food magazine, the next a health journal or entertainment guide, depending on an issue's primary or prospective source of ad revenue.

Whenever Altman and her sales team had difficulty convincing media buyers to place an ad, they blamed *American Profile*'s folksy, down-home content. If they were unable to sell ads based on the magazine's merits and rural demographics, they suggested that its content become more trendy and youthful, environmental or health conscious, and star-studded to attract advertisers. Or, they offered editorial favors to advertisers.

In 2003, Altman requested a story about softened water to accompany a Morton salt ad. "The Virtues of

Soft Water" explained the benefits of bathing and washing clothes with sodium-enriched water and ran next to a Morton System Saver Pellets ad. While appropriate and informational for homeowners with mineral-laden hard water, the story was far from celebratory of hometown life.

Food advertisers frequently requested adjacency to recipes that suggested—or mentioned—their products as ingredients. Ads for Bush's Best often flanked recipes that included beans; Cool Whip ads ran beside recipes that called for whipped topping; and a Sure-Jell ad in 2005 was published next to a Strawberry Freezer Jam recipe made with a box of Sure-Jell fruit pectin.

Occasionally, *American Profile* was transparent about its product endorsements. "One of our advertisers submitted this recipe for a tasty alternative to a traditional beef or pork hotdog," read the introduction to a Hometown Recipe from Odom Sausage Co. for Sausage Wedge Hotdogs, which included a pound of Odom's Tennessee Pride Country Sausage. The advertiser-supplied recipe replaced one from a reader.

Health stories tied to food ads often mimicked dieting fads and marketing trends, whether they promoted more calcium or less cholesterol, low carbohydrates or reduced sodium, or gluten-free products. For instance, a National Dairy Council ad in 2006 ran adjacent to a story titled "Five Tips to Bone Health," while "Foods that Help Your Heart" appeared beside a 2007 ad for Promise, a butter and margarine substitute touted "to help reduce cholesterol levels."

On occasion, a gung ho ad sales rep forced round pegs into square holes. In 2004, Altman requested a Hometown Spotlight to commemorate the 100th anniversary of French's mustard. She praised the ad salesman for "a great job incorporating marketing and edit" after he proposed the story—without consulting editors—in exchange for three French's ads. While Rochester, N.Y. (pop. 220,000), was the birthplace of the bright yellow condiment, the R.T. French Co. had vacated the city in 1987. Hometown Spotlights were supposed to be about small towns with good news or living legacies, not fading mustard memories in metropolises. Still, the story detailed French's roots in Rochester and ran in the same issue with a full-page mustard ad.

To avoid similar conflicts, Cox cleverly suggested new feature story categories, including Made in America and American Roots, to include products and companies with origins in the United States. The result was a proliferation of other feature categories, including American Artisans, Entertainment, Incredible Kids and Odd Jobs, and a shift away from Hometown Hero and Hometown Spotlight stories exclusively from small towns.

Altman publicly revealed her intentions to integrate advertising and editorial content prior to the 2006 launch of *American Profile*'s sister publication *Relish*, a monthly food magazine distributed via newspapers. "As long as your magazine is about entertaining and lifestyle, I don't think we should be held to the same standard as *U.S. News & World Report*," Altman told *Advertising Age*, which cited *Relish*'s plans to sell "brand mentions in recipes prepared by the editorial staff" and "product placement among staff-recommended kitchen and home gadgets."

Product placement reached a new high—or low, depending upon one's perspective—in 2007 with the launch of *Texas Profile*, a four-page addition to *American Profile* distributed exclusively in the Lone Star State. Sponsored by Ford Motor Co., the pullout required photo editor David Mudd to travel a half-dozen times to Texas, where he rented a Ford truck and strategically placed the pickup in photographs that accompanied stories with no relationship to Ford or its trucks. On one trip, Mudd drove to a remote crossroads called

Ford in the Texas Panhandle to photograph local ranchers and residents surrounding a Ford pickup for a story about odd-named places, including Bug Tussle, Cut and Shoot, Dime Box, Happy, Turkey and Uncertain. Though the U.S. automaker had no connection to the Texas crossroads and Ford wasn't a particularly peculiar name for a community, Mudd's photo "made the cover because we promised them (Ford Motor Co.) a cover," he said.

Mudd chose to photograph the advertising-driven assignments himself because he didn't want to expose freelance photographers to *American Profile*'s "shameless" product placement. "To me, it was embarrassing," he said. "It was like slipping them a Coca-Cola and saying 'Hold this.'"

Not all advertisers dictated or degraded stories in *American Profile*. Many merely paid for the space where their ads appeared, without a product mention or a companion story. Companies that made or marketed Bose audio systems, Duracell batteries, GEICO insurance, Henry rifles, Kubota tractors, Planters peanuts and Stihl chainsaws simply wanted to reach *American Profile*'s rural readership rather than change or influence its editorial content.

SOLD OUT

Some media buyers, however, insisted upon receiving editorial favors in exchange for an ad placement, or an ad sales rep offered a compatible story or product mention to sweeten or seal a deal. With its deep pockets, the pharmaceutical industry bought hundreds of pages of influence.

Chapter 16

Big Pharma

As *American Profile* weaned itself from cigarette ads, ads for prescription drugs, over-the-counter medications and health-care products proliferated, replacing and surpassing lost tobacco revenue.

Though *American Profile* wasn't a health magazine, the publication on occasion appeared to be one. It wasn't that newspaper publishers or readers had demanded stories about acid reflux or coping with incontinence. Rather, the company's top brass presumed that because drug companies bought so much of the magazine's paper and ink, they should determine some of its editorial content.

Pharmaceutical giants such as AstraZeneca, Bayer, Bristol-Myers Squibb, Eli Lilly & Co., GlaxoSmithKline, Johnson & Johnson, Merck & Co., Novartis, Pfizer, Roche, and Sanofi-Aventis purchased hundreds of ads in the general-interest magazine to the tune of tens of millions of dollars.

Like bloodhounds, ad sales reps followed the money, and Big Pharma, like Big Tobacco, had mega advertising budgets. Ad reps kept a keen eye on the release of new drugs, hoping to snag a portion of the proceeds from an initial marketing push. They also knew drug companies had plenty of products in the pipeline aimed at treating or preventing a plethora of conditions from arthritis to attention deficit hyperactive disorder (ADHD).

The first medical device and pharmaceutical ads adjacent to health stories appeared in *American Profile* in 2002. Initially, the stories were generic in nature and not directly tied to advertisements. Ads for the OneTouch Ultra blood glucose meter, for example, were published alongside stories titled "Keep an Eye on Your Vision" and "Managing Arthritis Pain." While ads for Glucovance, prescribed to control blood sugar for diabetics, were published with stories titled "Rx for Health: Back to Basics for a Healthful Life," "Ease Your Way to a Stress-Free Life" and "Health Tips for Men (50 and Over)."

As the pursuit of pharmaceutical revenue escalated, however, so did the link between drug ads and editorial content. *American Profile* published its first series of stories about diabetes in late 2002 beside ads for Avandia and Lantus, drugs used to treat Type 2 diabetes. The stories were titled "Managing Type 2 Diabetes" and "Outrunning Diabetes."

A single issue in 2004 contained ads for Bayer, St. Joseph and Ecotin aspirin, sandwiched between five health and fitness stories promoting heart health. The ads all touted a daily aspirin regime to maintain heart health and reduce risk of heart attack.

Not all drug ads required accompanying stories, but the number and frequency of editorial tie-ins gradually increased until the magazine was providing multipart series to some advertisers rather than individual stories. By 2008, nearly 60 percent of pharmaceutical ads ran adjacent to health stories or healthful recipes.

Under pressure to achieve and maintain profitability, Cox justified the practice, noting that other publications allowed advertisers to influence or dictate editorial content as well. He pointed to a dental health story next to an Oral B toothbrush ad in an October 2003 issue of *USA Weekend*. "I doubt if an editor even assigned this story," he said, suggesting that it may have been provided by the advertiser.

American Profile editors attempted to appease advertisers by offering regular health-related content on a variety of topics, from Alzheimer's disease to walking for fitness. However, media buyers eventually insisted upon—or were offered—stories specifically related to their drugs. This led to redundancy and displacement of stories with greater reader relevance or interest.

Between 2007 and 2014, *American Profile* published 30 stories about chronic obstructive pulmonary disease (COPD), ironically, caused largely by tobacco smoking. Most of the stories were accompanied by ads for Advair, Breo and Spiriva inhalers used to treat the disease that makes it difficult to breathe.

In 2010, *American Profile* began running ads for Gardasil, a vaccine used to prevent human papillomavirus (HPV), a sexually transmitted virus. Though the ads weren't accompanied by stories about HPV, they often were required to run adjacent to stories about children or parenting, since public health officials recommend that adolescents get the vaccine before they become sexually active.

While all prescription drug ads carried the fine print, hard-to-read product disclosures required by the U.S. Food and Drug Administration, none of *American Profile*'s health stories mentioned the potential adverse affects of the drugs, nor were parents asked if they wanted their children to appear in a story next to a Gardasil ad. The top priority was advertising revenue, not concern for readers, story subjects or their health.

Despite the proliferation of health stories, *American Profile* published few informational stories about cancer, the nation's second leading cause of death, presumably because pharmaceutical companies haven't developed a single pill to prevent or treat the disease's many forms.

Chapter 17
That's Entertainment

With the push to make *American Profile* more appealing to advertisers and media buyers, celebrity and entertainment coverage increased. In exchange for an ad, TV networks and music labels sometimes received a profile about a singer or leading actor, or mention of an upcoming show or album. The result was more Hollywood and less Main Street.

Despite Hammond's aversion to idolizing celebrities in the magazine, *American Profile* actually had a star-studded section from its inception. The Ask American Profile column allowed readers to submit questions about actors, singers, movies, TV shows, musical groups and professional athletes. Each week, the magazine answered three to five inquiries on Page 2, often providing accompanying photos of the famous people in question.

Hundreds of questions poured in from readers each month. "What can you tell me about the personal life of Chipper Jones, the Atlanta Braves' third baseman?" requested Guy V. of Ohio; "Whatever happened to Flip Wilson?" asked Marie Thorne of Norwalk, Conn.; "Kiss has always been my favorite band. What's up with lead singer Paul Stanley these days?" inquired Amy Astor of La Grange, Texas. Editors faithfully answered a small percentage of the reader inquiries.

American Profile didn't publish its first full-blown story about a celebrity until nearly a year after the magazine debuted. The subject was country singer and actress Dolly Parton, but even her identity was concealed on the cover. Titled "The Book Lady of Sevierville: Guess what famous person never forgot the kids back home," the story spotlighted Parton's program to reduce illiteracy in her hometown by providing free books to preschoolers in Sevier County, Tenn. A childhood photo of Dolly appeared on the cover, along with some of the books distributed via mail.

American Profile's guarded approach to celebrity coverage vanished with Hammond's departure. In addition to county music entertainers, the magazine in 2004 and 2005 published stories about TV host Charles Osgood, bluesman B.B. King, President Jimmy Carter, rocker John Mellencamp and romance novelist Nora Roberts, among others. Many of the profiled celebrities—particularly Christian evangelist Billy Graham, filmmaker Ken Burns and NASCAR legend Richard Petty—fit perfectly with the magazine's DNA.

SOLD OUT

Not all famous people, however, were so well received. An August 2004 cover story about Laura Bush was ill-timed prior to the November election of her husband, President George W. Bush. Some readers—particularly Democrat-leaning librarians—took exception to the first lady's comment about her former book-lending occupation ("It was one of the few jobs where you didn't feel guilty if you spend all of your time reading.") and the general timing of the story.

Keel and her successor, Neil Pond, former editor of *Country Weekly* and *Country America*, did a superb job as entertainment editors, covering famous people for readers enamored by celebrity. They also did a wonderful job serving entertainment advertisers by supplying promotional articles and planting questions from media agents and superstar promoters in the Ask American Profile column.

One dubious "reader" question, "What can you tell me about the Flame Worthy Awards?" appeared next to a full-page ad about CMT's *Flame Worthy Video Music Awards*. Attributed to John R. of Colorado, the inquiry received a comprehensive 400-word reply, the longest ever published on the Ask American Profile page and the only time a single question was answered.

That's Entertainment

Like Cox, Pond was an accomplished yes man, efficiently handling requests for stories and favors from the ad sales staff in New York, irrelevant of editorial autonomy or integrity. While he coined the catchy phrase "*American Profile* makes real people famous and famous people real," Pond was apt to overlook Average Joe and Jane, though he routinely performed public relations duties for Mr. or Ms. Celebrity when advertising dictated. For his contributions, Pond was promoted to editor in chief in 2008.

Editorial meetings led by Pond primarily were sessions to discuss advertising requests and requirements. Conversation generally focused on fulfilling the needs of the ad sales staff rather than brainstorming story ideas about the good news on Main Street.

When *American Profile* celebrated its 10th anniversary in 2010, Pond wrote an editor's note thanking readers for "the tremendous feedback, praise and encouragement we continue to receive about the 'good news' we bring you each week." All the while, he helped to undermine, reduce and replace that very content by kowtowing to advertisers via the ad sales staff.

Chapter 18
Double Standards

The absolute authority of advertising executives to control editorial content led to double standards: one for advertising, another for editorial. Not only did the duplicity create dissention among PGA employees, it modified the magazine's mission and gradually diminished the *American Profile* brand.

To impress Madison Avenue, marketing and sales executives requested stories about youthful, beautiful and famous people, especially on the cover. They found it difficult to sell ads when the magazine featured stories about the elderly, or people with unrecognizable faces or less than flattering features.

During a visit to PGA's Tennessee offices in 2008, Amy Chernoff, group publisher of PGA's print titles after Altman left the post, showed Mudd a copy of the "Encouraging Coaches" issue, which featured a cover photo of Mark Campbell, 59, a clean-shaven, gray-haired basketball coach at Claremore (Okla.) High School and a positive role model for his players. "This is exactly the sort of people we don't want on the cover," Chernoff told Mudd.

"Well, this is exactly who the story is about," responded Mudd, the photo editor.

Five years earlier, when the advertising staff launched its country music initiative, no one criticized a cover photo of wrinkled, scruffy-faced country singer Willie Nelson, though he was 70 years old at the time. Nelson was famous; Coach Campbell was not.

While first impressions are important, *American Profile* was intended to be about average Americans, not airbrushed supermodels or disheveled country music stars. Still, Sharp, the art director, did his best to make photo subjects more attractive. Combining his artistic talents and computer skills, Sharp administered digital facelifts and tummy tucks to make people appear younger or thinner. Occasionally, he trimmed hair, straightened teeth, or changed the color or style of clothing to create visual appeal.

Once, Sharp cropped Alan Jackson's hair and changed the color of his Western shirt. "Is that ethical?" asked Keel, looking at the modified photo of the country music star. "What about the ethical considerations?"

Neither Sharp nor Cox responded immediately, so Keel showed the "touched up" photo to officials of Jackson's management company. They were upset with the changes, she said, and didn't want the magazine's artist messing with their artist. On the other hand, Keel, a recording industry professor at Middle Tennessee State University, was aloof about the ethics of planting celebrity questions from publicists in the Ask American Profile column or publishing a torrent of country music-related stories to garner advertising revenue.

Average Americans, meanwhile, didn't have similar advocates at the magazine or publicists to pre-approve their photo makeovers prior to publication. And, in an ironic twist, while advertising and marketing executives paid painstaking attention to cover photos, they permitted hundreds of tacky and visually unappealing ads inside the magazine, including direct-response offers for brassieres, sexual dysfunction products and psoriasis cream, with images of the unsightly skin condition. In 2010, *American Profile* began publishing photos of children with cleft lips and palettes in ads for Smile Train, a charity that helps children with clefts and other birth defects, though without cosmetic surgery those children couldn't have smiled on the magazine's cover.

Since advertising ruled, readers and newspaper publishers who criticized the content of ads generally were ignored, even if those ads damaged the *American*

Profile brand and offended readers. To fill ad space and boost its bottom line, the magazine underwent a sexual revolution of sorts in 2004 by accepting ads for sexual dysfunction and enhancement devices, lotions and supplements. Despite periodic complaints from readers and publishers, more than 100 sex-related ads were published in the "family-friendly" magazine in subsequent years.

The repeated presence of sex-related ads indicated that enough readers were buying the products to justify their placement. Still, more than one person cited awkward moments when their young children or grandchildren inquired about the purpose of a Vacurect, a vacuum pump used to treat erectile dysfunction. Fortunately for schoolteachers who used the magazine's educational and historical stories as reading material for their students, none of the sexual-oriented ads required accompanying editorial content, such as "What is Sexual Dysfunction?" or "How to Use a Penis Pump."

While *American Profile* didn't oppose creating sexual education opportunities in homes and classrooms, the magazine in 2005 had an aversion to linking retired NFL quarterback Joe Namath to a sexual dysfunction product. Keel, the editor who interviewed the former

New York Jets player, suggested that a Vacurect ad be moved to a page with an article about the nation's poet laureate Ted Kooser rather than appear next to her story about Broadway Joe. She supported the change, arguing that Namath is better known than Kooser and the ad might perpetuate the football star's reputation as a playboy.

Altman approved the move, saying she didn't want sexual-oriented ads to run with cover stories. The Vacurect ad ended up adjacent to a Hometown Hero story about Bill Covitz, a Connecticut ice sculptor. Apparently, no one would suspect that a national ice-carving champion might be a playboy, or care if the little-known artist might be embarrassed being profiled on a page with a penis pump ad.

The move proved that *American Profile* had a double standard for celebrities and people of lesser renown. It also helped explain why Hammond had an aversion to celebrity stories and sexual-oriented ads.

While *American Profile* generally didn't prohibit seedy ads adjacent to stories, it made exceptions for one advertiser that wanted to avoid controversy and maintain a respectable image. Orrville, Ohio-based J.M. Smucker Co., the maker of jams and jellies, required four to six pages of separation between its ads and "sensationalized news, sex-related issues, violence, drugs (prescription or illegal), medicine, medical issues edit or ads, polarizing political issues, environmental issues, vulgar language, discrimination, religion, reference of games of chance, kid-targeted ads, and any alcohol or alcohol-related, including beer/wine/liquor/spirits edit or ads." Instead, Smucker's sought "synergy" near cooking stories and recipes.

Coincidentally, many of Smucker's strict ad placement guidelines were identical to Hammond's original advertising and editorial standards. Not many advertisers had such stringent guidelines. Nor did *American Profile*, except at an advertiser's behest.

The double standard applied to advertisers wasn't new. For example, some members of the magazine's advertising and marketing staff loathed a 2002 story about the Delaware Punkin Chunkin Association's 17th annual contest in Millsboro, which featured a cover photo of a middle-aged man holding a pumpkin with a trebuchet in the background. They considered the man a hayseed and the event hokum, not worthy of a cover story. However, seven years later, an ad sales rep requested—and was granted—a story about the same event to accompany an ad sold to the Science Channel, which aired back-to-back programs on Thanksgiving night about the pumpkin-hurling teams and their contraptions.

Double standards also applied to food and health matters. For instance, *American Profile* regularly published ads for calorie-, fat-, salt- and sugar-laden foods such as Ball Park franks, Kraft cheese, Milky Way candy bars, Pillsbury cookies, Tombstone Pizza, and McDonald's artery-clogging burgers and fries. Yet, in 2008, Cox announced that the magazine no longer would solicit recipes from its readers because complaints had been received that they were "too unhealthy."

Instead, recipes would be supplied by *American Profile*'s sister magazine *Relish*—which targeted urban and suburban audiences—in hopes that cosmopolitan and upscale cooks would submit more nutritious cuisine. The magazine's marketing executives and graphic designers also had complained that the low-quality snapshots supplied by small-town cooks made recipe pages look amateurish and unappealing. In addition, *Relish* editors often rolled their eyes when readers submitted home-style casserole recipes containing cream of chicken or mushroom soup, though Campbell's was a major advertiser in *American Profile* at the time.

Thus, Reader Recipes were phased out and often replaced with recipes from gourmet chefs, professional food writers and chic cookbook authors. Some of the new recipes had fashionable foreign names—Chicken Milano, Easy Posole, Gratin Dauphinois, Caprese Salad, Spanakopita Quiche—and exotic ingredients—arugula, Asiago, Gruyère, mascarpone, Parmigiano Reggiano—not commonly recognized or available in small-town grocery stores.

Gone were Aunt Rita's Potatoes, Hot Hominy Casserole and Oven-Fried Chicken. In were per-serving nutritional facts, gluten-free recipes and vegetarian entrees, though only about 1 percent of Americans suffer from celiac disease and 5 percent of Americans are vegetarians, particularly in cattle and hog country.

Elimination of Reader Recipes reduced reader involvement and diminished the homemade identity of the brand. The decision also disappointed—and perplexed—some *American Profile* admirers. "Have you stopped asking for reader recipe submissions?" loyal reader Marsha Baker asked. "I am one of the honored ladies who had several of my recipes published in your lovely little magazine, but the last few weeks you've had 'unusual recipes,' and I don't believe they come from readers."

"Please don't stop asking for readers to share their simple recipes," she added.

Despite such heartfelt pleas, the general consensus among PGA executives was that the financial health of the magazine depended on advertisers, not readers. Furthermore, if a story or recipe was requested for an advertiser, it was worthy; if it was submitted by a reader or written with readers—rather than profit—in mind, it was open to scrutiny and criticism. Therefore, editors willing to tolerate double standards and accommodate advertisers were most valuable to the company and were promoted accordingly.

Chapter 19

Damn the Firewall

While editors in Tennessee supplied the stories, advertising and marketing initiatives that originated in New York dictated much of the magazine's editorial content. Cox and Pond acted as intermediaries between advertising and editorial staffs, merging the company's creative and moneymaking functions so completely that they couldn't resist advertising's influence. The firewall, as it's known in the journalism profession, was battered and breached beyond repair, preventing *American Profile* from maintaining its integrity.

Each fall, as editors were compiling a slate of stories for the upcoming year, the ad sales and marketing team inserted a list of prerequisite stories and themes into the editorial calendar. The requested content followed the well-trodden trail of Madison Avenue ad initiatives and marketing budgets, explained the herd characteristics of the mass media, and diverted the magazine from its editorial mission.

In the first issue of January, a New Year's resolution story was requested to secure ads for smoking cessation or dietary products, supplements or low-calorie foods; Super Bowl-related content was mandated in late

January before the NFL's championship game; and NASCAR-themed cover stories were obligatory during the stock car racing season to woo prospective advertisers.

Annual breakfast and summer grilling stories were designed for food advertisers, as were Thanksgiving dinner and holiday baking issues. The back-to-school edition evolved into two consecutive August issues to entice advertisers such as Fruit of the Loom underwear, Oscar Meyer bologna and Wrangler jeans.

While some themed issues were extremely lucrative, others were financial flops. Between 2004 and 2014, *American Profile* followed the media herd, publishing 20 Super Bowl-related stories and "Big Game"-themed recipes. Yet, other than a few food ads, the magazine failed to capitalize on its requisite Super Bowl coverage.

Obligatory NASCAR coverage produced similar results. While *American Profile* published more than a dozen stories about NASCAR drivers, fans, pit crews and racing referees, the magazine sold limited advertising against the articles while reducing potential coverage of other pastimes and sports enjoyed by Americans. In response to repeated NASCAR story requests, Cox cited Albert Einstein's definition of insanity: "Doing something over and over again and expecting different results."

When it came to catering to advertisers, no story in *American Profile* was sacrosanct. Timely and time-sensitive articles frequently were relocated or rescheduled to accommodate an ad or prospective ad. In 2005, a story about the soldiers who guard the Tomb of the Unknowns in Arlington National Cemetery was scheduled to appear as the cover story in the Veterans Day issue. Instead, the story was published a week earlier to accommodate a Thanksgiving-themed story titled "Stuffing or Dressing?" assigned in hopes of attracting food advertisers.

A similar accommodation was made in 2011 after an ad salesman promised two cover stories, including one in the Veterans Day issue, to Wrangler to promote its National Patriot program, which raises awareness and money for the nation's wounded and fallen military veterans and their families. To retain a $1.5 million annual advertising account with Wrangler, the salesman initially proposed offering the Western apparel maker sponsorship of a scheduled story about Larry Eckhardt, an Illinois man who posts more than 1,000 American flags along the funeral routes of fallen soldiers. After editors complained that neither

SOLD OUT

Wrangler nor its program are affiliated with The Flag Man or his volunteer efforts, a story about country singer George Strait, a spokesman for the Wrangler National Patriot program, was assigned. The Strait story ran in the Veterans Day issue and the Flag Man story was published a week earlier. Celebrities 1, Unsung Heroes 0.

Takeaway: Preferential treatment for advertisers results in discrimination against average Americans.

Section V
DEVIL IN THE DETAILS

*

"The men who study the Bible with John Steeves aren't your average churchgoers. Dressed in orange prison garb, many await sentencing for burglary, trafficking in narcotics, rape or murder," wrote American Profile contributor Karen Karvonen.

"But that doesn't faze Steevees, a World War II veteran and volunteer minister from Neenah, Wis. (pop. 24,507). For nearly 45 years, he has spent three days a week sharing the Gospel and straight talk with inmates at the Winnebago County Jail in nearby Oshkosh."

"Some of them read and understand the Bible very well," said Steeves, featured as a Hometown Hero in 2007. "The trouble is they are good at talking about the Bible, but they aren't living it. I always stress that they need to walk the talk."

*

Chapter 20
Behind the Façade

Criminals don't have a monopoly on hypocrisy. While *American Profile* was proficient at profiling earthly angels and heavenly do-gooders on its editorial pages, the magazine's business practices were far from saintly or benevolent.

Behind the façade, PGA executives didn't adhere to the moral code they purported to support. The pages and soul of the magazine were for sale. Only insiders saw the underbelly of the beast.

Just as *American Profile* was generating significant and sustainable profits, PGA was sold in November 2007 to two private equity firms, reportedly for $126 million. The buyers included Boston-based Bain Capital Ventures, a subsidiary of its parent company co-founded by future Republican presidential nominee Mitt Romney, and Shamrock Capital Growth Fund, the investment arm of a Burbank, Calif., company founded for the late Roy E. Disney, nephew of entertainment and media magnate Walt Disney.

"We're buying a jewel in the media business," declared Paul Zurlo, a Bain Capital Ventures partner, in a press release. "The growth is available in magazines, digital and branded products, and we intend to push the throttle to take advantage of them all."

"PGA is a pioneer, and it can be a powerhouse," added Robert Perille, Shamrock's managing director. "PGA capitalizes on the underappreciated power of the hyper-local newspaper pipeline by complementing local news with special interest magazine content."

Porter, who announced the sale to employees via teleconference, said the new owners intended to grow the company, that few changes were planned in day-to-day operations and that no staff members would lose their jobs. "PGA stands now and always for integrity, customer service, quality and excellence in all that we do," he said.

The deal closed a month later just as the Great Recession was getting under way.

The timing of the sale was ideal for PGA's original investors and shareholders, who reaped a handsome profit and substantial financial windfall. Still, Hammond, who became a multimillionaire from his shares in the company, expressed doubts about the validity of the bidding process.

To avoid conflict of interest, Hammond had recused himself from the company's board of directors so he could tender a bid after he saw that initial offers were below what he thought PGA was worth. He claimed that he and a group of investors offered $140 million for the company, $14 million more the reported sale price. After failing to receive a response from the brokering agent on their original bid, Hammond said his group lowered their offer to $124 million, believing they would remain the high bidder. Their final offer, however, fell short of the price offered by Bain and Shamrock, which had joined forces to submit the winning bid.

Citing a request for him to remain in the lobby when his fellow investors toured PGA's Tennessee offices, Hammond believed Porter and Duggan didn't want him to regain the company he founded. "If I had gotten the company back, those two guys would have been fired," he added, calling Porter "a sniveling snake in the grass" and Duggan "a Judas."

As for the PGA sale, Hammond referred to it as "the day pride trumped greed."

Chapter 21

Ever-Shrinking Magazine

Almost from the beginning, PGA executives looked for ways to increase profits regardless of the interests and opinions of newspaper publishers and readers. The idea was *American Profile* could make even more by giving less. To cut expenses and improve the bottom line, regional content was reduced along with the magazine's overall size.

To save money on paper, ink and freight, the magazine's dimensions, or "trim size," were reduced at least a half-dozen times from its inception. The publication shrank incrementally, with slight horizontal and vertical decreases each time, resulting in shorter stories, and fewer or smaller photos. Overall, the ever-shrinking magazine lost more than 1½ inches horizontally and nearly 2 inches vertically. *American Profile* was a prime example of *shrinkflation*, in which the product gets smaller while its price remains the same. Company executives insisted the slight size reductions would be imperceptible to most readers.

Meanwhile, the percentage of space devoted to advertising increased. Just as the number of ad-driven stories was proliferating, Porter devised another way to

Ever-Shrinking Magazine

"monetize editorial"—by selling products and services directly to readers. "Too bad our readers don't pay for the magazine," he remarked. "It would be great if each reader sent us 10 cents."

Because the company's business model didn't allow readers to subscribe to the magazine, Porter conceived publishing internal promotions to reap revenue from readers. In 2005, Porter hired Steve Minucci as director of business development to sell travel packages, books, CDs, DVDs and an assortment of other products through "house ads" in PGA's magazines. Minucci's first internal promotions were for *American Profile* cookbooks, followed by offers for ice cream makers, Lawrence Welk CDs, slow cookers, Veggie Tale DVDs, fresh Christmas wreaths, Randy Travis CDs and first-aid kits. Before long, *American Profile* was offering Bible verses, horoscopes, jokes, weather forecasts or recipes via cell phone for $9.99 a month, as well as dental and vision insurance plans.

By extracting dimes and dollars from the pockets of readers, PGA racked up more than $1 million in additional revenue during its first year of publishing house ads—all the while delivering shorter stories and smaller photos in *American Profile*.

Many of the house ads had direct or indirect links to stories, such as a 2007 article about the Statler Brothers quartet with an offer for their recently released *Random Memories* book, or a cowboy music CD offer on the same page as a Hometown Spotlight about Lockhart, the Barbecue Capital of Texas. Because house ads usually ran on the same pages as the associated articles, they didn't reduce the number of other ads in the magazine, though they sometimes required stories to be cut and photos to be cropped. With ads, promotions and editorial tie-ins constituting up to 70 percent of some issues, *American Profile* at times resembled an advertising circular interspersed with a few stories.

Readers seldom commented on the ads, unless to report that they hadn't received a product from a direct-response vendor, or to criticize their placement or preponderance. In 2006, Pamela J. Meyers complained that excessive advertising made the magazine mostly a waste of time. "Any magazine that is 16 pages in length and nine of those pages are advertising, I am not interested in," she wrote. "This is obviously a venue for advertisers only; not a public service."

When questioned about sacrificing editorial content to accommodate advertising, Porter said the company had to walk a fine line between securing ad revenue and remaining relevant to readers. He noted that some publications were taking drastic measures to stay in business, including slashing budgets and staffs amid declining rack sales and a highly competitive advertising environment. To make his point, he showed the staff the February 2007 edition of *More* magazine, featuring a cover story about actress Diane Keaton and an inside advertisement for a L'Oreal skin care product for which Keaton was a spokeswoman. "This is what she (Altman) has to compete with," he said, suggesting that most people don't mind the link between advertising and editorial content. After mentioning other examples of product promotions embedded in magazines, TV shows and movies, Porter said he hopes advertising never infiltrates the news.

In fact, advertising was supplanting the good news in *American Profile*.

Chapter 22

Austerity Measures

PGA's new corporate owners faced their own financial concerns immediately after buying the company. The Great Recession that began in December 2007 foretold challenging and transitional times for the publishing industry and the nation. Triggered by a real estate market collapse fueled by fraud and excessive debt, the financial crisis led to hundreds of bank failures, a stock market meltdown, a marked decline in advertising spending and austerity at PGA.

During a staff meeting in March 2008, Porter said the company was facing economic headwinds, including rising paper costs and declining brand advertising, particularly from the pharmaceutical industry. In response, cost-saving and profit-enhancing measures were implemented, including trimming the size of *American Profile* and *Relish*, and increasing the previously balanced ad-to-edit ratio to 60-to-40. The latter, Duggan said, was necessary to help finance debt assumed when Bain and Shamrock bought the company. The tactics were akin to tossing crucial cargo overboard to float a leaky boat, and some sailors began to jump ship.

Austerity Measures

In June, Duggan left PGA for New York-based Alpha Media Group, which published *Maxim* and *Blender* magazines. Within a few months, he recruited seven PGA employees to join him at Alpha Media's offices in Franklin, Tenn. Duggan was replaced as CFO by Bob Brolund, who represented himself as a corporate turnaround specialist. In September, Altman announced her departure for *Reader's Digest* and was replaced by Chernoff, previously associate publisher. In October, controller Greg Coble also resigned.

Despite the economic downturn and employee turnover, PGA weathered the onset of the recession fairly well. The company actually increased ad sales and hired four new employees to launch its third newspaper insert, *Spry*, a health and fitness magazine targeting women. Bob Mattone, a former *TV Guide* sales manager, was named *Spry* publisher and Lisa Delaney, previously executive editor of *Health* magazine, was hired as editor in chief.

While other magazines were failing and folding, *Spry* debuted in September 2008 with a monthly distribution of 9.2 million, shattering circulation records for a magazine startup. "*Spry* shatters the myth that there is no room for mass-distributed magazines anymore," said Husni, who bestowed PGA with its third magazine launch of the year title. "*Spry* provides clear evidence that a well-targeted, special-interest publication, can and will make it in today's marketplace."

While Mr. Magazine's remarks were flattering, the realities of the economic recession began to set in. Not only did overall print advertising suffer a steep decline, but PGA's three print titles began competing with one another for the shrinking pool of ad revenue. The rich times following the sale of PGA turned lean.

Some readers and publishers began to notice the austerity measures, which resulted in fewer stories, a higher percentage of advertising and smaller magazines. "I am disappointed in the *American Profile* magazine that I always read. It's just real small and it is smaller than what you've had before," said Joann Anderson of New Mexico in 2009. "I'm disappointed in the format of the magazine. Why you did this I don't know. It's not even interesting to read anymore."

The changes were particularly apparent when *American Profile* shrank to 12 pages, ad-driven articles replaced "good news" stories and cover stories ran in the back of the magazine to accommodate ads in the front. Advertising mandates resulted in chaotic page layouts, multiple story jumps (as many as three in a 16-

Austerity Measures

page magazine), and frustration and inconvenience for readers.

"I was very interested in your story in the April 20-26, 2008 edition about ancestral search and wanted to make a copy to read again later," said Carolyn Weir of The Villages, Fla. "That story was spread out on so many pages, printed both horizontally and vertically on different pages, that I had a terrible time cutting it out and piecing it together. It was in seven pieces and was like a puzzle."

Weir added: "I realize your advertising is important, but can't you put your stories together better than that? I'm sure some people probably got tired of it and just threw it away."

In 2010, Romaine Smith of Sherwood, Ore., voiced similar annoyance. While she enjoyed reading "The Inspiring Story of Our National Anthem," she detested its segmented layout, which included two jumps over five pages. "Why didn't you present it as a special section, no advertising and continuous as a booklet so parents could preserve it for our children and grandchildren to read? How irritating it is when ads dominate the paper," she wrote.

While *American Profile* editors and designers were sympathetic to such reader feedback, they couldn't and

SOLD OUT

didn't implement any changes. Financial considerations dominated and advertising directives ultimately dictated the magazine's content and page layout.

Chapter 23

Window Dressing

Because PGA's advertising executives consistently cited *American Profile* stories and images as the problem when ad sales lagged, they were convinced that the magazine would benefit financially from a fresh look and approach. Thus, the publication underwent periodic makeovers in hopes of attracting advertisers.

Amid the economic recession and advertising dearth of 2009, Cox introduced a magazine redesign and a new motto "Celebrating the American Spirit," which replaced the original "Celebrating Hometown Life" and subsequent "Celebrating the People, Places and Things that Make America Great."

Despite prodding from editors for more specifics, Cox declined to define the American spirit, preferring to leave the catchphrase open to interpretation for branding and marketing purposes. However, he did say that future stories should be relevant to both advertisers and readers because some perceive the magazine's appearance and editorial content as "old-fashioned" and "homespun." He encouraged editors to ask: "Is a potential story relevant to our readers? Is it relevant to our advertisers?"

A few months later, Cox came under fire from Brolund and Lyles for allowing advertisers to dictate editorial content, in particular the ill-conceived placement of a Travel Channel ad promoting its reality TV series "Man v. Food." Though editors grumbled about the multi-segmented ad, it was published as directed, strewn across a profile about NASCAR driver Mark Martin, cluttering the layout and making the story difficult to read.

Readers also complained. "While it was a good article, I feel that the advertisement for Travel Channel's 'Man v. Food' was ill-placed and took away from the article," wrote Sharon Verone of Rio Rancho, N.M. "I can't actually believe someone thought this was a good idea. Please rethink advertising placement for articles in the future."

Criticism about the dissected story made company executives realize that the ad had gone too far. During a subsequent meeting to discuss editorial and production standards, Cox acknowledged that running the fragmented ad was a mistake. "The Travel Channel ad violates everything we're trying to accomplish editorially," he said.

During the same meeting, editors discussed setting limits and reestablishing a boundary between advertising and editorial departments. Pond proposed creating three pages of "sacred space" in each magazine—two for the cover story and one for a feature story—devoid of ads or advertising requirements. Cox admitted that allowing the advertising and marketing staff to dictate editorial content and page design had "morphed into a business model." "Monetizing every page only works in catalogs, not magazines," he added.

Regardless, Cox and Pond rarely championed the editorial mission they were charged with overseeing. As executive editor, Cox could have denounced the overwhelming influence of advertisers, though he seldom did because he refused to challenge Porter. "I'd just as well jump out of this window," he said, motioning to the glass pane of his fourth-floor office. As a compliant functionary, Cox was resigned to work for a catalog.

During editorial meetings, Pond often used sarcastic quips when announcing advertising directives that he was tasked with implementing. His wry humor and accommodative talents, however, did not translate into bold editorial leadership. "At least we all still have a job," he was fond of saying.

SOLD OUT

Not all employees were so reticent. Lyles, who was responsible for selling *American Profile* to newspapers and increasing circulation for all three of PGA's titles, regularly questioned Porter's decisions and the direction the magazine was headed. He also conveyed the concerns and criticisms of newspaper publishers who carried the magazine.

Some publishers were disappointed with *American Profile* for eliminating or reducing regional content and stories about hometown America; some complained about cigarette ads, sex-related product offers or ads from Walmart, which competed with their own hometown clients; some were concerned about losing their discounted postal rate because of the magazine's rising ad-to-edit ratios; and others grimaced at having to pay for 12-page publications loaded with ads, advertorials, and repeated stories about COPD and diabetes, while *Parade* was distributed free.

Hundreds of newspapers stopped carrying *American Profile* for failing to live up to its promises or for no longer providing value to them. Some canceled the magazine and began inserting *Parade*. "You can't continue to give them less and expect them to be satisfied," Lyles said, claiming that PGA had "prostituted or whored" itself to advertisers and showed little concern for newspaper publishers who paid to distribute its magazines.

After years of frustration with his concerns falling on deaf ears, Lyles resigned in July 2009 to join Duggan and other former PGA employees at Alpha Media Group. One of the last—and strongest—advocates for newspaper publishers, readers and editorial integrity was gone.

Following Lyles' departure, *American Profile* in 2010 attempted to rein in the influence of pharmaceutical advertisers by publishing a "Making U.S. Healthier" series, featuring stories on a variety of health topics, including asthma, multiple sclerosis and schizophrenia. However, as the recession subsided and ad sales picked up, the magazine returned to 16 or more pages and proposals to limit the influence of advertisers fell to the wayside.

In October 2010, *American Profile* published its fourth annual three-part series about COPD, which both disappointed and provided comic relief for the editorial staff. When a cold-suffering editor coughed, others joked that she probably contracted the chronic lung disease from the sheer number of COPD stories published in the magazine. Actually, it was no laughing matter to watch the self-induced deterioration

SOLD OUT

of a once beloved and pioneering magazine—despite the cosmetic makeovers and window dressing.

Takeaway: Beware the devil in disguise.

Section VI
DIGITAL DIVIDE

*

"With practiced fingers, Lois Csontos-Nielsen feeds the tattered edge of a U.S. flag into her sewing machine. Stars and stripes emerge from the other side as good as new—ready to fly again over the graves of soldiers at Ohio Western Reserve National Cemetery in Rittman (pop. 6,314)," wrote American Profile *contributor John Gladden.*

"Each Friday for the last 10 years, Csontos-Nielsen, 76, has packed up her sewing machine in nearby Sharon Township and driven to the cemetery to volunteer her time. Dozens of flags await her attention—along with the occasional stray button on the uniforms of veterans who perform military honors at funerals."

"I keep a little emergency sewing kit here," said the modern-day Betsy Ross, profiled as a Hometown Hero in 2010. "There's always a little mending to do."

While Csontos-Nielsen was honoring the nation's military veterans by repairing frayed American flags, financial concerns were impairing PGA's moral fiber and dismantling the magazine established a decade earlier to celebrate unsung heroes like the patriotic seamstress.

*

Chapter 24

Tangled and Twisted Web

Because print magazines were struggling and presumed destined for the dustbin, PGA's owners steered the company into the technological future. In August 2010, Brolund announced Porter's departure, saying that the board of directors decided to make a change in leadership to expedite its digital initiative.

John Cobb, former senior vice president of digital at Source Interlink Media, replaced Porter as CEO and quickly hired a team of digital hotshots to usher PGA into the 21st century. His goal was to increase online traffic and advertising revenue by redesigning and upgrading the company's websites, creating new ones and introducing other digital products. To fund the undertaking, the company funneled millions of dollars in profits from the print publications to hire digital marketing executives, website designers and editors, and social media consultants.

While some employees hoped that Cobb would return editorial integrity to the company, he soon revealed that his business philosophy was similar to that of his predecessor. During a staff meeting five months after he was hired, Cobb remarked that PGA "has a great system" that is "far better than other media companies" in terms of cooperation between advertising and editorial staffs. Using his hand to illustrate his point, Cobb said most publications have a distinct barrier between editorial and advertising departments. "That's not the case here," he said, referring to the company's long-fractured firewall.

Cobb's frank remarks foreshadowed that the slippery ethical slope constructed and greased for the print publications would be extended online. Moreover, *American Profile* readers would remain largely irrelevant—except to click on online ads and provide personal marketing data—in the push for digital profit.

During a digital training session, consultant Kevin Richards instructed PGA editors to no longer reply to readers' calls, letters or emails, describing electronic mail as "old technology." Instead, he suggested posting all answers to readers' questions on Facebook or Twitter, though not all *American Profile* readers had computers or social media accounts. He encouraged editors to use social media to attract online followers and to build a virtual "community." He also advised editors to take advantage of their "celebrity" status by posting personal information on Twitter. As a possible tweet, Richards suggested: "I'm munching on carrots while waiting at the dentist's office."

Such directives dumbfounded editors who previously had tried to respect readers by responding to them individually. Being instructed not to reply to them reinforced their insignificance, and being advised to embrace social media as a way to build "community" seemed ridiculous while ignoring individual readers in the thousands of communities where *American Profile* was distributed. Likewise, encouraging editors to masquerade as carrot-munching celebrities illustrated how far PGA in general—and *American Profile* in particular—had strayed from its original editorial mission: to celebrate the "good news" in small towns and pay homage to average Americans.

During a subsequent meeting, Richards said that once marketing opportunities were identified, editors should produce content that generates advertising revenue. "Where we're going to be putting our effort is . . . based upon our ability to sell content," he said, adding that the goal was to exploit "the value of (online) real estate" and "invest resources in sold-out sections." In other words, editors would become online marketers, producing stories with Web-based search engines in mind, rather than for longtime readers of the print magazine who embraced and identified with the *American Profile* mission and brand.

In early 2011, PGA launched its three redesigned websites—*americanprofile.com, relish.com* and *spryliving.com*. In hopes of driving traffic to *americanprofile.com*, Pond advised editors to stop referencing other websites in print stories, even if such references could benefit readers. Meanwhile, *American Profile* tried to drive traffic to its Facebook page with repeated "We're on Facebook" blurbs on the magazine's cover. The magazine wanted to be "liked," though possibly for the wrong reasons. Three years later, *American Profile*, with a weekly circulation of 10 million, had 33,000 Facebook "friends," which was a social media failure based on potential numbers.

Despite a few glitches and blunders—including incorrect ingredient measures in online recipes (attributed to outsourcing work to a company in India), a search function that didn't work and failure to identify states in tens of thousands of state-based trivia—PGA's leadership heralded the upgraded websites as a grand success, even though staff members had difficulty navigating them and finding online content that they knew existed.

Tangled and Twisted Web

Digital director Matt Arceneaux, who supervised the website overhauls, struggled to explain why their attractive and visually stimulating pages loaded annoyingly slow. Their sluggishness must have discouraged repeat visits, especially among rural dial-up surfers without access to high-speed Internet. Arceneaux several times claimed that he had remedied the problem, though the slowness persisted on *americanprofile.com* until hundreds of archival stories—dating to the magazine's birth in 2000—were removed from the website.

Rather than providing virtual access to all of the stories and photos previously published in *American Profile*, PGA purchased and posted hundreds of generic stories written with Internet search engines in mind. The Helium Network, an Andover, Mass.-based media content provider owned by PGA's printer RR Donnelley, supplied the stories. While topics such as "How Can I Lose Weight?" "Makeup for Men," "What is Vinegar?" and "How to Pitch a Softball" helped bolster PGA's online content database, the lightweight-as-air articles made *americanprofile.com* a directory of random information as much as a portal for "celebrating the American spirit."

SOLD OUT

Incredibly, all of the Helium-produced stories carried bylines by Randall Stokes or Avery Mann, fictitious names conceived by PGA employees for unknown Helium writers. Not much could be expected of stories with bogus bylines and uninspired headlines such as "How to Fold Napkins," especially since nameless Helium writers earned pennies per word, whereas *American Profile* paid freelance contributors 50 cents to $1 a word and reimbursed them for travel expenses. Helium announced its shutdown in 2014, noting that its "business model cannot be sustained."

Still, with online content available for a pittance, Brolund said PGA no longer could afford to pay $1,000 for a cover story in the print magazine, even though an *American Profile* writer might travel to multiple states and conduct dozens of interviews to complete a wide-ranging, 1,000-word story. How else could the magazine have produced original, on-the-scene articles about individuals tracing their ancestors to the U.S. Immigration Station on Ellis Island, hikers who completed the coveted Triple Crown of America's long-distance treks, or four industrious American families that built and lived in medieval-style castles? Meanwhile, the brief, bargain-basement articles purchased from Helium seldom mentioned people or personal accounts.

In January 2012, Pond instructed editors to reduce by 10 percent rates paid for stories and photographs that appeared in *American Profile*, though the budget cut did not apply to content purchased exclusively for the website. He said "bean counters who sign the checks" thought freelance contributors were paid too much. Predictably, the company's bean-counting executives considered all content essentially the same, particularly if it garnered equal or greater advertising revenue. Plus, they didn't know precisely what was in *American Profile* because they seldom if ever read the publication. They presumed they knew the book by glancing at its cover.

How could they know if *American Profile* was fulfilling its editorial mission if they didn't read the magazine? They couldn't and didn't. Bean counting was their mission; the quality and content of the magazine was largely irrelevant as long as ads were plentiful and beans were abundant. As advertising and editorial became intertwined online, the technological turn taken by PGA contributed to a tangled and twisted Web.

Chapter 25

Robots vs. Humans

While the *American Profile* brand was based upon inspirational stories about real people and authentic places, the quest for advertising revenue prompted PGA to turn to digital scams and Web-based tricks to boost online traffic. Because organic human traffic wasn't increasing fast enough to suit company executives, PGA began purchasing traffic, some of which mimicked legitimate ad clicks and views. In 2012, Brolund said the company earned "a good return on investment" buying traffic, spending $100,000 to receive $500,000 in revenue.

By taking advantage of cyber tricks and computer robots, or bots—as they're called in Internet circles—PGA joined a shady group of digital media companies engaged in deceptive and fraudulent tactics. "Fraudsters, working in cahoots with crooked publishers, are making a fortune ripping off advertisers for millions by sending bogus traffic to websites and generating phony clicks on ads," according to a 2014 promotion for a free informational webinar on click fraud sponsored by BPA, a media auditing service that validated circulation of PGA's print magazines each year.

Aided by bots and gimmicks, PGA's website traffic grew to "millions of hits" a month. Company officials discussed reducing traffic purchases, but the easy money was too enticing and digital schemes became an integral part of PGA's business model. In 2013, Pond said the majority of *americanprofile.com*'s traffic was purchased.

A 2014 article in the *Wall Street Journal* estimated that 36 percent of all Web traffic is bogus. The Interactive Advertising Bureau (IAB) claims that click fraud undermines the entire online advertising industry because brands waste money on ad campaigns and lose confidence in digital media. "In addition to . . . diverting payments from legitimate businesses to fraudulent ones, traffic fraud also impacts the integrity of digital media," according to the IAB. So while brand advertisers were tarnishing the credibility of print media with planted stories and product placements, digital media was diminishing the integrity of online advertising by employing computer robots and digital trickery. The result was a perfect example of what comes around goes around, as both gradually lose the trust of their audiences and consumers.

SOLD OUT

American Profile had other legitimate—though likely not as lucrative—ways to boost Web traffic, including promoting original online content in the magazine and via the social media networks of people, businesses and organizations mentioned in its stories. Editors created exclusive online content and published links in the magazine to encourage its millions of readers to visit *americanprofile.com*. Digital editor Sherry Phillips, however, often failed or refused to post the promoted content—stories, slideshows and videos—to coincide with the magazine's weekly release. It wasn't a priority for her or her bosses, preoccupied with launching blogs and e-newsletters, experimenting with QR codes, and creating apps and tablet editions.

Instead, Phillips concentrated on applying search-engine optimization (SEO) techniques to headline writing and keyword phrases to boost online traffic. Sometimes the Web-based tactics—and trickery—came with a price: deceptive and inaccurate headlines. Guided by search-engine analytics, Phillips rewrote headlines, occasionally inserting words with no relationship to the stories. For instance, a story about a team of artists who in 2011 painted a series of old-fashioned murals on the walls of buildings in downtown Plymouth, Wis., was posted with the headline "Artists Decorate Town With Vintage Advertisements—Mad Men-style murals illustrate Wisconsin town's history on brick walls and barns." The headline was misleading because the TV show *Mad Men* wasn't mentioned in the story and the outdoor murals had no relationship to the 1960s Madison Avenue advertising agency depicted in the award-winning AMC series. Plus, no barns were painted in Plymouth.

Accuracy wasn't paramount among the yes men and women with editor titles. Cox justified the headline revision, saying *Mad Men* was a popular show and the keywords were required for SEO, so online surfers for the phrase would "hit" the website. He didn't see a problem with the revised headline because the story and *Mad Men* both were about historical advertising. Presumably, neither robots nor humans would care if headlines were bogus.

One altered headline cast a group of college students as "crazy" for their chosen professions, presumably because "crazy" was a popular and trending search word. A 2013 story about "Uncommon College Degrees" was rewritten online as "10 Crazy College Degrees," implying that students in the article either were academic eccentrics or schizoid scholars for studying the bagpipes at Carnegie Mellon University in Pittsburgh, Pa., training to be a farrier at Mesalands Community College in Tucumcari, N.M., or learning to be a citrus grower at Florida Southern College in Lakeland.

American Profile, which previously avoided intentionally offending its readers or insulting story subjects, wasn't opposed to lowering the bar to drive traffic to its website. In fact, Cox argued that different editorial standards existed for print and digital stories. While online headlines should be "mechanically accurate," they needn't be "philosophically" accurate, he claimed. In other words, words should be spelled correctly and sentences should be grammatical, but headlines need not precisely reflect the content of a story.

To attract Internet surfers, editors were encouraged to produce Web-friendly slideshows, videos and "list" stories, such as "America's Best Beaches: From Sea to Shining Sea," "20 Memorable Veteran's Day Quotes," and "Top 10 Fireworks Displays in America." Even if stories weren't written as lists of superlatives and their authors used no ranking criteria, Phillips recast them as such at the behest of Web consultants and online marketers, including her boss, Arceneaux, who was not a journalist. An *American Profile* story titled "Countdown to New Year: Americans celebrate with descending fruit and carp kisses" became "Top New Year's Eve Drops" online, "Waterparks: Making a Splash" was re-titled "Best Waterparks in America," and "Stargazing: Five super places to view the night sky" was relabeled "5 Best Stargazing Spots in America." Whether an event or place was among the "best" really didn't matter, as long as the superlative claim attracted Internet users.

Cox justified the online headline revisions, saying *American Profile*'s digital traffic was increasing due to SEO and print editors shouldn't concern themselves with "philosophical problems" on the website. A programmed human was promoting robotic traits. By rationalizing inaccurate and misleading headlines, Cox sloshed another bucket of oil on the slippery slope, smearing the website's credibility and the brand's integrity.

Declining ethical standards led to apathy and lackadaisical attitudes, which resulted in sloppy online editing, ridiculous errors and an inferior website. In 2013, one slideshow on *americanprofile.com* misspelled President Obama's first name and identified John F. Kennedy as JKF. At the request of other editors, Phillips

SOLD OUT

reluctantly corrected those errors, though she frequently disregarded other mistakes, deeming them too trivial or time-consuming to fix.

Chapter 26
Breakdown Breakup

With digital business clearly the focal point, PGA's print titles suffered financially, editorially and aesthetically. By 2012, the company's sales team could barely sell a brand ad in *American Profile* without providing a health story to a pharmaceutical advertiser or planting a celebrity question in Ask American Profile whose answer referenced an upcoming TV show.

A challenging environment for print advertising and competition with digital media weighed heavily on the company's bottom line. With fewer high-revenue brand ads, the number of lower-revenue direct-response ads increased, as did the ad-to-edit ratio, resulting in shorter, dissected stories and mediocre magazines. Some 16-page issues contained a single feature story.

While Brolund maintained that *American Profile* remained the "backbone of the company" and that it would be "in the foreseeable future," the company's primary focus was growing its digital business. As a result, PGA's flagship magazine was considered yesterday's news.

Cobb, who had been hired for his digital expertise, wasn't particularly fond of print media, including the newspapers that carried PGA's magazines, although those papers provided the distribution network that enabled the company's founding. Bolstered by shifting media trends, his partiality and single-minded focus became evident in 2012 as PGA's rising digital revenue—even if obtained fraudulently—exceeded its print revenue for the first time.

PGA's owners couldn't allow the fiscal deterioration of the print titles to continue. In July 2013, the company's digital and print components were severed in hopes of strengthening—or saving—both. The exclusive rights to publish PGA's three print titles—*American Profile, Relish* and *Spry*—were acquired by Nashville-based Athlon Sports Communications, reportedly for $1, with Athlon assuming PGA's multiyear printing contract with RR Donnelley. PGA—also known as PGOA Media—retained its digital properties. For marketing purposes, PGA was identified as PGOA Media beginning in 2009 to distinguish it from the Professional Golfers Association (PGA) of America.

"The genius of our agreement is simple: Each partner will be able to focus on what they do best while joining forces to create scale and reach for our advertisers," said Athlon COO Chuck Allen in a press release. "This will enable Athlon to continue to harness and broaden the strength of its print properties allowing PGOA to further develop and broaden its digital brands."

Speaking to the editorial staff the day after the announcement, Allen attributed PGA's breakup to an attempt to allow its corporate owners—Bain and Shamrock—to recoup some of their financial losses, since the average return on investment for digital properties was 7 to 12 percent, compared with 4 to 5 percent for print media.

Cobb and Brolund attempted to put a positive spin on the breakup of the company they headed. "Athlon is a great partner for PGOA Media at this time, enabling us to extend our reach to important segments of the marketplace while we continue to invest and develop our existing digital properties," Cobb said. "It's a nice synergy, enabling both of us to leverage all of our assets."

Brolund said the split would create "two companies with one link—content. Both will be better served."

While hailed as a win-win, the decision to partition PGA's media properties confirmed that Cobb and Brolund had failed to maintain the economic viability of the overall company. The breakup was due to financial breakdown. Eight employees were laid off, while retained employees were divided, based on their specialties, between Athlon's Nashville offices and PGA's digital operations in Franklin.

Athlon, which produced the newspaper-distributed monthly *Athlon Sports* among its 15 sports-related titles, soon was renamed Athlon Media Group and became the nation's largest publisher of newspaper-delivered content with circulation of 43 million via 1,600 newspapers.

During a subsequent meeting with print staff, Cox—among the employees transferred to Athlon—handed out T-shirts that read, "I think we have an opportunity" amid an atmosphere of hopeful uncertainty. "Ask not what your company can do for you, but what you can do for your company," he said, paraphrasing JFK.

While the separation was dubbed a partnership, the relationship between Athlon and PGA was more akin to a married couple who lived in different homes and communicated primarily for the benefit of their children. Their bonds were contractual and obligatory rather than practical and heartfelt.

A human link, however, did exist between the companies as four former PGA employees, including Lyles, worked for Athlon. "We hope to get *AP*

(*American Profile*) back to its roots," said Lyles, who became Athlon's vice president of publisher relations after a brief stint with Alpha Media. A proponent of *American Profile*'s original editorial mission, Lyles told Pond that the magazine's "ad sales people don't need to be concerned with the editorial content of the product, only the demographics" of its readers.

He added: "A 28-year-old media buyer in New York is not going to read *American Profile* anyway. We need to focus on the rural C and D counties. I don't care if we're called hicks or rednecks."

The rift between Main Street and Madison Avenue reappeared—along with a familiar sales executive from *American Profile*'s past.

Chapter 27

Severing the Roots

In hopes of reviving PGA's languishing print titles, Lyles recommended that Athlon hire Altman to head advertising sales, with the stipulation that the editorial mission and integrity of *American Profile* be restored and maintained. Allen took Lyles' advice. Within four months of the split, Altman was Athlon's chief marketing and development officer.

In November 2013, Altman returned to the print titles—*American Profile*, *Relish* and *Spry*—that she had left in 2008 for executive stints at *Reader's Digest*, *Parade* and *Dash* magazines, respectively. "Tracey will operate across all brands and titles and be instrumental in developing 'selling proposition,' branding and positioning of our products," read an Athlon corporate announcement. "Tracey is proficient in both operational and strategic initiatives and understands content, advertising relationships and the needs of our 1,600 newspaper partners."

A month later, Pond unveiled Altman's "strategic planning initiative" for *American Profile*, which reflected some of the priorities supported by Lyles and editorial staff members. The initiative called for:

1) More editorial space for the cover and feature stories, including a two-page "cover spread," through a reduction in the magazine's advertising-editorial ratio, with plans to attract more brand advertisers and requiring fewer direct-response ads;

2) A return to Reader Recipes, submitted though a contest, to increase reader involvement;

3) A once-a-month health story series, with useful information beyond diabetes and COPD, to accommodate prospective pharmaceutical advertisers; and

4) Improved "iconic" covers to serve three audiences: readers, publishers and advertisers.

Altman also introduced an editorial platform titled "The Kindness Project" tied to the magazine's annual Acts of Kindness story. She requested more stories about kids, such as the magazine's Incredible Kids feature, and a travel series. Pond said Hometown Spotlights and Places stories, accompanied by state maps, would fulfill the latter requirement. As for appearance and overall mission, Pond said Altman approved of 80 percent of the magazine's cover images and believed *American Profile* "is doing lots of things right and there's no need to change the DNA of the magazine."

Editors cautiously embraced Altman's initiative, aware that she was at the helm a decade earlier when the firewall between advertising and editorial was breached and *American Profile* began its long slide down the metaphorical slippery slope. In January 2014, Altman introduced a new motto—"Celebrate, Smile, Inspire"—and a new "marketing strategy," which she said takes the magazine "back to our roots." She said the magazine would profile "celebrity farmers and ranchers," and publish stories about hiking, fishing, hunting, crafting, scrapbooking, American traditions and patriotic themes. "We got away from our roots and what is important about our brand," she said during a PowerPoint presentation via teleconference, adding: "Community newspapers are the heart and soul of the community." She also stated that the magazine had to be careful with editorial tie-ins, such as repeated COPD stories, because it's "not good for the brand or the advertiser to be too overt."

Cox said Altman's strategy provided *American Profile* with "a new spin" and ability to "reposition *AP* in the eyes of the advertising market," adding "the goal is more ad pages while not abandoning what we are doing" editorially. He urged editors to get behind Altman's initiative "110 percent."

Severing the Roots

Within a week of unveiling her "back to our roots" initiative, Altman's insincerity was revealed when Pond, acting as her messenger, announced the need to make changes to the magazine's upcoming story lineup to be more accommodative to advertisers. He also announced that *American Profile* no longer would publish Hometown Spotlights, a regular feature since that magazine's inception that focused on small towns across the nation. Also eliminated were Made in America stories about U.S. manufacturers and profiles featuring Americans with unusual occupations. Altman cited reader research data for implementing the changes, though she didn't share the information with the editorial staff for analysis.

Altman's decision to eliminate Hometown Spotlights revealed her disregard for the communities where *American Profile* was distributed. Upcoming stories about Bedford, Ind., the self-proclaimed Limestone Capital of the World, and Sedalia, Mo., the Cradle of Ragtime music, were canceled, though their community newspapers, *The Times-Mail* and *The Sedalia Democrat*, carried the magazine. No longer would *American Profile* shine the limelight on the small towns and cities that had contributed to its success.

SOLD OUT

While Altman's goal was to return *American Profile* to profitability, her approach was anything but patriotic. Her ban on Made in America stories prohibited articles about small family- and privately owned manufacturers dedicated to keeping their operations in the United States. No longer would the magazine profile companies such as Deering Banjo Co. of Spring Valley, Calif., the largest banjo manufacturer in the nation; Kepner-Scott Shoe Co. in Orwigsburg, Pa., the oldest children's shoe manufacturer in the United States; William Marvy Co. in St. Paul, Minn., the last manufacturer of barber poles in North America; or Waterbury Button Co. in Cheshire, Conn., which has manufactured buttons for the U.S. armed forces for more than 200 years.

Meanwhile, *American Profile* regularly granted editorial favors to multinational corporations such as Kimberly-Clark, Tyson Foods and VF Corp., whose Kleenex facial tissue, chicken breast fillets and Wrangler jeans ads touted "available at Walmart," the retail behemoth and longtime nemesis of family- and independently owned stores in small-town America.

Though she may not have realized or cared, Altman's editorial decisions undermined the American dream and economy by disregarding the small towns, businesses and people that *American Profile* originally uplifted and celebrated. Embracing the prevailing U.S. corporate business model, her strategy pitted the interests of Main Street against global conglomerates, the Wall Street financiers that lend them money to expand overseas and the Madison Avenue hucksters who peddle their products. She sold the soul of *American Profile* in a desperate attempt to save the magazine.

Systematically, Altman and her subordinates dismantled the magazine by removing its editorial pillars. Before long, the last of the magazine's original story categories and regional content was eliminated. Rather than returning *American Profile* to its roots, Altman had severed them.

Chapter 28

Some Things Never Change

Altman's abrupt flip-flop wasn't completely unexpected. She long had attributed the sales team's inability to sell brand ads to *American Profile*'s editorial content, which she considered flawed and unsophisticated for appealing to senior citizens and rural readers. After convincing Allen that the outmoded magazine had to be revamped to restore profitability, Altman and her subordinates frantically searched for a new look and engaging approach that they believed would attract a younger audience and more advertisers. Some of their ideas were considered harebrained by editorial staff; others simply sounded silly.

To make the magazine more visually attractive, Cox proposed running iconic photos of America—not associated with any inside article—on the front page, seemingly forgetting that the magazine had published hundreds of stunning cover images related to stories since its inception. His bold idea lasted for three issues.

Cox asked editors to "re-imagine the mission of the magazine." "I want to have a new look at where we want *American Profile* to be," he said, adding that stories need to have "more personality," a "different voice and tone" and to be "current and relevant" to readers, publishers and advertisers. "The magazine needs to change quickly because the financials (advertising revenue) are not there," he said. "We can't continue to do what we're doing and be successful."

During a subsequent meeting, Cox distributed a story about hot chicken wings published in *The New Yorker* magazine. He cited the story as an example of being "conversational" and "different in tone," overlooking its expletives and the fact that the upscale, urban newsstand magazine was distributed to an entirely different audience than that of family-friendly *American Profile*.

In an attempt to make the magazine more contemporary, Pond suggested eliminating stories with historical themes. "I don't think old American history—the American Revolution, the Civil War and World War II—is relevant" to readers, he said. Only "modern history" of 50 years or less is relevant, he added, failing to explain how *American Profile* was to celebrate the nation's holidays, icons, legacies and traditions without mentioning their origins or past.

When asked about a story published marking the 50th anniversary of President John F. Kennedy's assassination, Pond said that "worked for us" because there was a "buzz and excitement" about the commemoration, suggesting that historical events only are pertinent if covered by other mainstream media. Pond felt safe with the herd and made exceptions for ads hawking products pertaining to earlier American history, such as a half-dollar coin commemorating the 70th anniversary of the Japanese attack on Pearl Harbor and *The Civil War*, a documentary film by Ken Burns.

While *American Profile* was undergoing a fundamental editorial transformation, Altman's approach to selling ads was the same old story. Altman, who headed ad sales in 2003 when *American Profile* ran a cover story commemorating the 100th anniversary of Ford Motor Co. in exchange for a lucrative four-page ad, was back in charge in 2014 when the magazine published a nostalgic cover story marking the 50th anniversary of the Ford Mustang. Unfortunately for her, Ford didn't buy an ad to accompany the Mustang article and the story didn't generate any coveted ad revenue.

Such was not the case with stories about COPD and the CMT Music Awards, which ran adjacent to ads for a breathing inhaler and the annual country music awards show, respectively. Two Pall Mall cigarette ads also appeared in *American Profile* in 2014, the first in more than a decade. In short, the more editorial content changed, the more advertising scruples and tactics remained the same.

Still, Altman continued to consider editorial content the problem and was determined to retrofit the magazine to attract brand advertisers. To make her point, she cited a 2013 Starch Advertising Research study that identified the typical *American Profile* reader as a white, college-educated 44-year-old woman with a household income of $72,400—an ideal demographic for brand advertisers. Simultaneously, many of the magazine's direct-response ads—for adult diapers, medical alert buttons, hearing aids, oxygen therapy devices, stairlifts and walk-in safety tubs—targeted older readers.

"That is a result of the content," claimed Delaney, who in March 2014 was named editorial director of *American Profile* and *Spry*, replacing Cox as executive editor. "The impression we leave, due to the images we use and the content we feature prominently, is that we are a magazine for older readers, which handicaps our ability to attract brand advertisers who are, for the most part, not interested in marketing to older demos."

SOLD OUT

Since most brand advertisers didn't target seniors citizens, Delaney reasoned that *American Profile* shouldn't either, even though the magazine continued to publish—and earn considerable revenue from—ads aimed at folks with arthritis pain, hearing loss, hot flashes, incontinence, wrinkles and other woes that accompany aging.

Shortly after being hired by Athlon, Delaney announced a change in the magazine's editorial direction. Though she didn't provide a specific mission statement, she indicated that the magazine no longer would focus on Americana or celebrating the people, places and traditions that make America great. Instead, she spoke of transforming *American Profile* into a "consumer magazine," replete with product endorsements rather than stories about the Americans who invented the products or the companies that made them. She emphasized "family-oriented" and parenting issues, with a focus on advertisers such as Elmer's and Kraft. However, she rejected a story about homeschooling in a back-to-school issue as "too polarizing," as if homeschoolers don't consume cheese and use glue.

For a fresh start, four longtime *American Profile* editors were laid off and replaced by employees who would help create a publication with contemporary appeal. During the magazine's transition, its big-city counterparts—*Parade* and *USA Weekend*—faced their own financial difficulties. In September, Athlon purchased *Parade* and *Dash*, a newspaper magazine with a focus on food, from Advance Publications. In December, *USA Weekend* ceased publication, citing declining demand for print advertising.

Despite employee turnover, marketing initiatives and editorial changes, Athlon struggled to sell brand advertising as well. With a practical monopoly on the newspaper magazine market, Athlon in January 2015 consolidated its titles and downsized distribution. *Dash* was discontinued and merged with *Relish*; *Parade*'s weekly distribution was reduced to 22 million from 32 million; and publication of *American Profile*—renamed *American Profile's Community Table*—was cut to twice a month and its circulation slashed to 6 million from 9 million, requiring cancellation of newspapers that had carried the weekly magazine since its birth.

"Athlon is where it all will die," said Hammond, predicting the end of the publication he founded to celebrate the "good news" in hometown America.

During Athlon's makeover of *American Profile*, Cox and Delaney both said readers have changed since the magazine debuted. Delaney said the magazine must "stay current" and change with the times, adding that its readers are different than they were 10 to 15 years ago. Both were correct.

More Americans are impoverished, unemployed and receiving federal assistance than when the magazine was launched in 2000; terrorism and war are more prevalent; more Americans are overweight and on antidepressants; trust in the U.S. government and mass media has declined; Americans are farther in debt and the nation's disparity in wealth has increased since *American Profile* was named co-Launch of the Year.

What Cox and Delaney overlooked is that what's great about America is timeless and worthwhile, especially during tough economic times. While good news may be harder to find, it remains meaningful and valuable. That never changes.

Takeaway: If U.S. publishers do some soul-searching, they'll discover that they—and the nation—could use a lot more good news, whether it's delivered digitally or in print.

AFTERWORD

What happened at *American Profile* and its parent company isn't unique. Short-term financial pursuits and unscrupulous business practices are commonplace in corporate America. That doesn't make them sustainable or right.

The rise and decline of *American Profile* in many ways represents a microcosm of what has transpired across the United States during the last three decades. Main Street went from a place of eternal hope, prosperity and locally owned businesses to a place of internal decay accelerated by globalization and Wall Street greed.

When U.S. manufacturers moved their operations overseas, vacant buildings replaced bustling factories and Americans were resigned to buy inexpensive foreign-made products. When Walmart and the big-box stores came to town, mom-and-pop shops closed, downtown business districts faltered and many small-town publishers sold their newspapers to corporate media chains. Soon payday lenders moved in to prey on the poor and unfortunate.

When the Information Age arrived, many Americans traded corporate-owned newspapers and magazines for Asian-made flat-screen TVs and smartphones. The Madison Avenue ad agencies that developed marketing campaigns for the multinational corporations began ditching print for digital media. By the time the Great Recession hit in 2007, the downward spiral was nearly complete as PGA and other companies took drastic measures to make money and remain in business.

Ironically, *American Profile* was both a perpetrator and victim of the economic trends and realities. The magazine—founded to celebrate the best of hometown America—eventually embraced some of the worst business practices of Wall Street and debt-laden corporations. Similar to banks and mortgage companies that lent money to borrowers who couldn't repay the loans, or bankrupt General Motors, which ignored automobile design flaws though its customers were dying in car crashes, PGA's irrational and unethical practices were driven by greed or short-term profit.

Seeking a solution to the conflicting interests of advertisers, readers and partner newspapers, Cox suggested that *American Profile*'s business model might be flawed. Actually, it was Cox, Pond and other followers who made the magazine's three-legged stool defective because they didn't have the courage or devotion to support their leg. Like go-along congressmen who keep voting for deficit spending, they feared losing their jobs more than standing steadfast on principle.

Lyles claimed the business model wasn't flawed, just poorly executed. He was correct. When ad salesmen and accountants took the reins of the company, the vision of producing a unique, relevant and high-quality magazine was lost. Other than as a moneymaking tool, Altman, Porter and other company executives failed to have confidence in *American Profile,* or great concern for its ultimate customers—the readers. Rather than requiring advertising to be sold based on the magazine's audience and merits, they allowed its integrity to be compromised and reputation to be tarnished. "They just don't *get* it," Lyles said.

Hammond concurred. He said the business model got out of balance when the people who replaced him focused solely on short-term revenue and forgot a basic media tenant. "Readers, subscribers and viewers are not stupid," he said. "They see through nonsense in a nanosecond, and when they become doubtful or no longer trust the brand, it's a self-fulfilling prophecy, a spiral downward."

The paradox is that the U.S. corporate business model is flawed for relying too heavily on borrowed money, focusing primarily on short-term profit, and rationalizing disingenuous or fleeting concern for customers.

If Hammond made a mistake, it was launching *American Profile* with capital supplied by company-flipping Wall Street investors who cared little about the long-term viability of a magazine that celebrated Main Street, and for hiring key executives who didn't share his vision or valued money and corporate ladder-climbing more than the product they were selling.

By allowing advertisers to exert excessive influence, PGA and other media companies with similar lopsided business models are committing slow suicide. Once advertisers and marketers control 100 percent of what we read, hear and see, will anyone pay attention to the endless ads, commercials and product pitches? If magazines publish full-page ads on every cover, will more readers flock to the newsstand? If CNN airs around-the-clock Coca-Cola commercials, will anyone tune in? Should NASCAR driver Danica Patrick sport a GoDaddy tattoo on her forehead? Even advertising reaches a point of silly saturation.

To thrive and survive, all businesses—including magazines, newspapers and digital media—must earn a profit. The cost of financial gain, however, shouldn't be the loss of common sense. Without good judgment and personal integrity, a private business enterprise can't be socially responsible—and ultimately should fail.

ABOUT THE AUTHOR

A 1984 graduate of Indiana University, Stuart Englert worked as a newspaper editor, investigative reporter and feature writer in Indiana and Idaho before he moved to Tennessee and helped launch *American Profile* in 2000. He worked for the magazine for 14 years, serving as both Midwest and senior editor.

www.ingramcontent.com/pod-product-compliance
Lightning Source LLC
Chambersburg PA
CBHW031050180526
45163CB00002BA/771